Praise for *Trauma and the Unbound Body*

"This groundbreaking book teaches us how to resolve all levels of trauma through inhabiting the internal space of our body. The practices and teachings reveal the ground of fundamental consciousness, and Judith Blackstone is a brilliant, experienced guide. This path of healing trauma is deep, powerful, and true."

TARA BRACH, PHD
author of *Radical Acceptance* and *True Refuge*

"Judith Blackstone works at the junction point between pure awareness and our own messy physical and emotional selves. She teaches embodiment at a very deep level, and in this marvelous book, she offers a step-by-step process for healing trauma through embodied awareness. Blackstone's Realization Process can help you discover the fundamental wisdom within your body—within the bones, the muscles, the fascia. The more you tune into this fundamental ground, the more awareness itself can begin to release the effects of psychological and physical wounding. This is psycho-spiritual work at the cutting edge of freedom!"

SALLY KEMPTON
meditation teacher and author of *Awakening Shakti*
and *Meditation for the Love of It*

"*Trauma and the Unbound Body* is a cutting-edge book which elegantly shows us how spiritual awakening enriches bodywork and psychological healing. Judith Blackstone begins with a clear exploration about how we organize ourselves in response to trauma. She then shares examples and practical methods for attuning to fundamental consciousness to release trauma-based patterns. Both healers and those healing will cherish this book!"

LOCH KELLY, MDIV, LCSW
author of *Shift Into Freed*

T0053890

"Judith's book is a powerful, practical guide to working with trauma. She helps the reader reclaim lost qualities such as power and voice through the practice of inhabiting the body and the ground of being that is our natural birthright. This book is a truly helpful guide for those who have experienced trauma to disentangle from challenging experiences and to attune to their body's healing potential that is available in each moment."

KELLY BOYS
author of *The Blind Spot Effect*, mindfulness trainer with the
United Nations Foundation, and host of *Mindfulness Monthly*

"*Trauma and the Unbound Body* is an exceptionally clear, finely tuned, and innovative guide for understanding and healing the divisive impacts of trauma. By deeply inhabiting our bodies—entering into the subtle core and attuning with an inherent fundamental consciousness—we discover that our true nature is both unique and non-separate. Judith Blackstone is a real pioneer in the emergent field of embodied awakening. Highly recommended!"

JOHN J. PRENDERGAST, PHD
author of *In Touch* and retired adjunct professor of
psychology, California Institute of Integral Studies

TRAUMA <small>AND THE</small> UNBOUND BODY

Also by Judith Blackstone, PhD

Belonging Here:
A Guide for the Spiritually Sensitive Person

The Intimate Life: Awakening to the Spiritual
Essence in Yourself and Others

The Enlightenment Process:
A Guide to Embodied Spiritual Awakening

The Empathic Ground: Intersubjectivity and
Nonduality in the Psychotherapeutic Process

TRAUMA AND THE UNBOUND BODY

The Healing Power of Fundamental Consciousness

JUDITH BLACKSTONE, PHD

sounds true
BOULDER, COLORADO

Sounds True
Boulder, CO 80306

This book is not intended as a substitute for the medical recommendations of
physicians, mental health professionals, or other health-care providers. Rather, it is
intended to offer information to help the reader cooperate with physicians, mental
health professionals, and health-care providers in a mutual quest for optimal well-
being. We advise readers to carefully review and understand the ideas presented
and to seek the advice of a qualified professional before attempting to use them.

Published 2018

Cover design by Jennifer Miles
Book design by Beth Skelley

Printed in the United States of America

BK05521

Library of Congress Cataloging-in-Publication Data
Names: Blackstone, Judith, 1947- author.
Title: Trauma and the unbound body : the healing power of fundamental
  consciousness / Judith Blackstone, PhD.
Description: Boulder, CO : Sounds True, [2018] |
  Includes bibliographical references.
Identifiers: LCCN 2018008808 (print) | LCCN 2018013064 (ebook) |
  ISBN 9781683642084 (ebook) | ISBN 9781683641834 (pbk.)
Subjects: LCSH: Psychic trauma—Treatment. | Psychotherapy.
Classification: LCC RC552.T7 (ebook) | LCC RC552.T7 B53 2018 (print) |
  DDC 616.85/210651—dc23
LC record available at https://lccn.loc.gov/2018008808

10 9 8 7 6 5 4 3 2 1

CONTENTS

INTRODUCTION

THE UNDIVIDED LIGHT

To know all things, including the painful and
difficult, are lit from within by undivided light.

AURA GLASER

Wholeness is not a vague ideal, but a lived experience. It is
a potential, inherent in our human nature. To be whole
is to be conscious and in contact with ourselves everywhere in our body, to live within our body. When we inhabit our
body, we experience ourselves as an undivided consciousness, a subtle,
unified ground of consciousness, pervading our whole body and our
environment, at the same time.

This book offers a method, called the Realization Process, of understanding and healing trauma. To heal means to become whole. Trauma
fragments and limits our wholeness. In the following chapters, I will
show how trauma separates us from our body, how it disrupts the
unity of body and mind and the oneness of self and other, and how we
can resolve this separation.

When we embody our wholeness, our thoughts, emotions, sensations, and perceptions occur as a unity. Our senses function as
a unity. Our actions spring from a single source of understanding,
emotion, and physical sensation. Even the smallest movement of our
body, as we turn our head or gesture with our hands, carries the full

breadth of our human capacities. So, for example, we can experience love and intelligence in our arms or our legs; we can hear with our whole body, heart, and mind.

To be in contact internally with our body is, at the same time, to be open to our environment. Everywhere that we are in contact with ourselves within our body, we are alive and responsive to the world around us. This produces a lived experience of continuity and connection with everything and everyone that we encounter.

Yet, even though this fundamental, unified ground of our being is right here, as simple to reach as living within our own body, most human beings never experience it. Even though our basic nature is wholeness, somehow we become divided. This is because the traumatic events that occur in all human lives cause us to fragment and diminish our ability to live fully within our body.

There are two categories of trauma: extreme events, such as severe injury or abuse, that impact us with great force, and relational trauma that everyone faces, especially in childhood, when ordinary events are too abrasive or confusing for us to fully absorb them. In general, relational trauma consists of small painful events that are repeated over time, while extreme trauma can occur just once in order to have a lasting impact on us. Both types of trauma have a shattering effect on us. In reaction to traumatic events, both big and small, we constrict and fragment our body and withdraw our consciousness from those parts of our body. We organize ourselves in ways that dampen the impact of intolerable experience or that restrain those aspects of our own behavior and personality that have brought us harm.

We can probably all understand how being held down and sexually assaulted or severely beaten by a gang of assailants on the street can have a lasting effect on our psychological state. It may not be so easy to grasp that ordinary, seemingly insignificant events, especially when we are very young, can impact our experience for the rest of our lives.

Here is an example. An infant is nursing at her mother's breast, and then, feeling contentedly sated, pulls away from the breast and begins to drift into sleep. But abruptly she is woken by the anxious mother forcing her breast into her mouth, compelling her not only to swallow the unwanted milk, but also to absorb the mother's anxiety about feeding her new baby and the sense of rejection and abandonment that the mother felt when her baby pulled away. We can see that there is no blame here. The mother is mal-attuned, but her anxiety, even her sense of rejection, are understandably human. However, in an attempt to keep out the unwanted milk, the baby naturally tightens her throat. She may even constrict her chest in order not to feel the mother's emotional upset. These are natural, spontaneous movements of protection against unpleasantness and overwhelm. However, if these tense, mal-attuned feeding events are repeated over time, the infant's protective patterns will become chronic tensions in her throat and chest. As she gets older, feeding may become increasingly fraught, due to the pattern of tension in her throat and her associations of emotional upset with taking in food. When she grows up, this tension may still affect her eating habits. She may feel some vague, apparently inexplicable anxiety at mealtimes. She may even experience another person's attempts at affection as intrusive. She may also harbor a static, background belief about herself that she has done something wrong or hurt someone in some way that she cannot clearly point to but that nevertheless leaves her feeling not quite innocent.

These patterns of constriction and belief form throughout childhood, in relation to our immediate family and to our peers at school. We also constrict ourselves in reaction to abrasive sensory stimuli in our environment. The constant presence of cigarette smoke in our childhood home may cause us to inhibit our breathing; the persistent racket of traffic or passing trains may cause us to impede our hearing.

Although most relational trauma occurs in childhood when we have less perspective with which to assimilate events and less freedom to leave traumatic circumstances, as adults, we can also be traumatized by ongoing abusive relationships or by overwhelmingly painful events. Someone who is consistently denigrated, for example, by a spouse or a boss at work may react in the same way as a child does to an abusive sibling or adult, by forming lasting beliefs about themselves and others and creating chronic bodily patterns of constriction that express these negative beliefs or that protect against the full impact of the abuse.

Because children also mirror the patterns of constriction in their parents' bodies, we embody not only our reactions to our own trauma, but we take on some of our ancestors' reactions to their trauma as well. This is one of the ways in which trauma is passed down from one generation to the next.

Our history of trauma, bound within our body, may haunt our present life as chronic feelings of sadness or despair, as distracting bouts of fury, or as spells of terror. But it can also be present as numbness, as a chronic static in our perception, as if we were always slightly removed from ourselves and our surroundings. This pain, whether it be conscious suffering or that slight sense of unreality, is often mistaken for our basic nature, something we just need to shoulder or ignore in order to move on. But it is not our basic nature. Just as an open hand is hidden within a fist, our true nature, with its innate capacities for happiness, love, and wisdom, is hidden within our pain and numbness. Just as we can open a fist to reveal a hand, our unbound, unconstructed being can emerge from our pain and breathe again. Within the complexity of trauma-based beliefs and constrictions, we can find our unbound body and the wholeness that is our birthright. We can experience ourselves as the one light, the undivided consciousness, that is the ground of our being and of all being.

A Process for Healing and Wholeness

The Realization Process is a series of practices that I have developed and taught over the past four decades. Its effectiveness has been proven to me consistently over this time, both in its application to my own healing and to the healing of the many people who have come to work with me. These practices approach the healing of trauma in two ways. There are practices that directly facilitate body-mind integration through inhabiting the internal space of one's body, attuning to the unified ground of fundamental consciousness and the inherent qualities of one's being that emerge as we know ourselves as this ground. And there are practices that utilize our attunement to fundamental consciousness in order to precisely and lastingly release the trauma-based constrictions in the body. This release, in turn, enables us to more fully inhabit the body so as to become more whole within ourselves and more open to our environment.

When you inhabit your body, you do not just return to the relatively unguarded, unfragmented state of early childhood. To come back into the body in this conscious way produces an experience that is probably not available to most children and that has rarely been mentioned in the field of psychotherapy. It is the experience of yourself and your environment as pervaded by or "made of" the subtle undivided consciousness that I call "fundamental." By applying fundamental consciousness to the healing of trauma, we enter territory that has traditionally been called "spiritual." For this reason, in the Realization Process, psychological healing and spiritual awakening are considered to be two intertwined and inevitable aspects of our progression toward personal maturity.

I cannot make any definitive metaphysical claim about fundamental consciousness, because I do not know what it actually is. Descriptions of what seem to be this same experience appear in Asian spiritual teachings, especially within certain Hindu teachings, such as Advaita Vedanta and Kashmir Shaivism, and the Buddhist teachings of Mahamudra and Dzogchen. However, there is much variation in the interpretations of this experience within spiritual literature. Some Asian teachings say that this ground of consciousness is our own individual mind, our own awareness, that we are perceiving along with the objects of our perception. Other teachings claim that it is the ground of our being, our "Buddha-nature" or Self (Sanskrit: *Atman*). Still others say that fundamental consciousness is the underlying nature of the whole universe and that when we know ourselves as this consciousness, we are realizing the true nature of the universe.

I do know that the experience of fundamental consciousness is available to us. It appears to be a given aspect, an innate potential, of our human nature, in much the same way that love is.

When you experience fundamental consciousness pervading your whole body, you experience the internal coherence of your individual being. You do not need to create this unity or integration—it occurs spontaneously. It feels like the deepest contact that you can have with your own existence. When you experience this same fundamental consciousness pervading your body and environment at the same time, it is also the basis of the deepest, truest contact that you can have with other people and with all forms in nature. It makes yourself and your environment a spacious oneness, without eradicating in any way the substantiality and separateness of your individual being. In this way, it is an experience of oneness and separateness at the same time. Through my years as a teacher and therapist, I have found that finally knowing yourself as fundamental consciousness is crucial for psychological health.

As a method of psychological healing, the Realization Process can be classified as a body-oriented, relational, transpersonal psychotherapy. However, it is not an amalgam of these various approaches. It grew from its own root in the rich field of psychotherapy, bodywork, and spiritual modalities. The approach presented in this book differs from other methods of healing from trauma in several key ways.

It is a body-oriented approach to healing from trauma because of its emphasis on the psychologically based, bound patterns in the body. Most of the popular methods of body psychotherapy today focus on the flight, freeze, or fight functions of the nervous system that may become chronically activated in reaction to extreme stress and trauma. In contrast, the Realization Process focuses on the shaping of the whole body in reaction to trauma, even the relational trauma of ordinary but painful, repetitive childhood events. In this way, we can uncover the exact pathways with which we constricted ourselves and gain insight into the psychological history that shaped us.

It is most likely the fascia of the body that is the shaper of the body in reaction to trauma. Fascia is the connective tissue in the body that surrounds all of our bodily structures. Our fascia is itself a dimension of wholeness. It is made of interconnected tissues that reach everywhere in our body. In the living body, it is a fluid medium that appears to react to both physical and emotional stresses, and then harden, over time, into those reactive shapes. Although this requires more research to establish scientifically, there is a great deal of anecdotal evidence to suggest that the fascia stores the emotional charge of trauma and even the memories of the trauma, or at least, provides access to those memories. In this way, working with the fascia provides a comprehensive approach to releasing trauma from all aspects of the physical body, as well as releasing emotions that are held in the body, and bringing to awareness the memories and beliefs associated with the traumatic events so we may resolve them. The nervous system naturally relaxes into its parasympathetic mode as well, as we release the constrictions within our whole body.

The Realization Process also focuses on more subtle facets of the body—energy and consciousness. Since these aspects of ourselves do not submit easily to scientific scrutiny, they are not often included in the body psychotherapies of our scientifically oriented culture today. Yet, as you will see in the following chapters, they are experienced as primary aspects of our being and therefore play a crucial role in our healing from trauma. The Realization Process provides a method for refining and deepening our inward contact with our body in order to contact and live within these more subtle aspects of ourselves.

Like many current transpersonal methods of psychological healing, the Realization Process aligns itself with the category of spiritual teachings called "nonduality." But "nonduality" is an umbrella term that encompasses a variety of spiritual perspectives, including those teachings that recognize a ground of being and those that do not. The Realization Process differs from most nondual psychotherapies because it includes a sequence of attunement practices for uncovering the experience of subtle, unified consciousness throughout our whole body and environment.

The Realization Process is also distinct from most nondual teachings in that it does not consider nondual realization to be the eradication of the experience of individuality. Many current nondual psychotherapies aim to minimize a person's sense of individual existence, including their capacity to think and feel, and their embracing of their personal history, preferences, and aspirations. But in the method presented here, we see that the realization of ourselves as fundamental consciousness actually deepens and matures our inward contact with ourselves, rather than eradicating it. It heals and deepens all of our human capacities.

Many of the spiritually oriented people who come to work with me ask if meditation is sufficient for becoming whole or if we can release the constrictions in our body that obscure that wholeness without knowing our personal history. I believe that healing does not occur, or last, without psychological insight. We need to know our history in order to find and release the exact pathway of our trauma-based constrictions. We also need to become conscious of the unconscious memories and beliefs that color our perception of ourselves and our environment, and that influence our choices.

If you do not understand the situations that led to your patterns of constriction, you are also more likely to reorganize them whenever similar situations arise in your life. You need to know, for example, if you constricted yourself in terror as a young child in reaction to a violently angry parent because as an adult, you may avoid or feel terror when confronted with even minor conflicts with the people close to you. But if you understand the exact relationships that produced your patterns of constriction, you will be able to remain open and responsive in your present-day life and relationships.

Finally, the Realization Process is a relational therapy because it understands that we fragment and limit ourselves, mainly in childhood, in relation to the first people we love and rely upon. Healing these fragmentations necessarily recalls the challenges of these early relationships. Like most relational psychotherapies, it views the cultivation of our capacity for authentic connection with others to be one of the hallmarks of psychological health. But it diverges from most other relational models because it sees the ways we have limited ourselves as not just mental events, but as patterns that are bound within the tissues of our body. Also, it specifically applies the realization of fundamental consciousness to helping people heal their relational wounds. Because this consciousness is experienced as pervading ourselves and others at the same time, it can open us to the pleasure of experiencing oneness with another person without losing the safety of inward contact with ourselves.

Developing the Realization Process

When I began to develop the Realization Process in the early seventies, I had not yet trained as a psychotherapist or discovered the budding fields of transpersonal psychology and contemporary spirituality. I had not yet begun my studies of Asian philosophy or recognized that I was on a path of spiritual awakening. The early versions of the practices that I include in this book came to me as I lay on the floor of my loft in lower Manhattan. I was badly injured, struggling to recover from disastrous surgery on my spine, and grieving for the loss of my career and my agility as a highly trained modern dancer. The surgery had left me with the feeling of a dense brick in my lower back. All of the methods of healing that I had pursued had been unsuccessful at dissolving this rigidity. I felt abandoned by the medical profession, by the alternative healing professions that I had tried, and by my own previous good fortune. So I was desperate. I lay on the floor and focused within myself, as deeply as I could, looking for the key that might free me from this seemingly insurmountable situation. And little by little, I found it.

I discovered that if I dropped my weight to the ground, currents of energy seemed to arise from the floor and move my body toward balance without any effort on my part. I also found that the more I refined my inward focus within my body, the more I could feel streaming energy within my body.

When my focus finally reached the innermost, vertical core of my body, I entered a realm of experience that was even more subtle than energy, that felt like a primary ground of consciousness pervading my body and even all of the objects around me in my room. I found myself in a transparent world where I experienced my own being and everything in my environment as both solid and permeable at the same time, as if made of consciousness itself.

I also discovered other rigid places in my body that resembled the experience of the brick in my lower back. They were places where I could not contact myself, that did not move with my breath. They felt rigid and thick. I found that if I focused within them in a particular way, they began to unwind. They were not completely static.

They were constrictions, frozen movements of protection that contained within them the exact movement of their release. They were parts of myself that I had squeezed shut. The unwinding process brought to my awareness memories and emotions from my childhood, and even the feeling of myself at younger ages.

After my injury, I still made my living giving dance classes in my loft, as I had always done when I could dance. This meant that every few days, I had to get up off the floor and face a group of people who were expecting me to teach them something about movement. I began to teach them what I was learning about the subtle aspects of the body. I saw that as they began to more fully inhabit the internal space of their bodies and find these more subtle aspects of themselves, it enriched their movement. Their bodies became more balanced, fluid, and expressive. They seemed to glow from within. In this way, the Realization Process emerged not just in response to my own particular problems but to the needs of my students as well, as it continues to do today.

During those early days of healing and teaching, I had a dream that I did not yet understand. I dreamt that I was entering and moving across the stage in a slow dance. The stage and theater were completely dark, but my body was made of light. I was to discover that within the body is this underlying unity, this one light, that can reach into the trauma-laden rigidities and fragmentations in our body and heal them.

In This Book

This is my sixth book on the Realization Process, but it is the first to focus specifically on applying the Realization Process practices to healing trauma. I begin with a detailed description of how we organize ourselves in reaction to trauma. Then, in chapter 2, I write about the experience of knowing ourselves as fundamental consciousness and the qualities of our being that emerge with this realization. In chapter 3, I describe how inhabiting the body contributes to healing by providing internal unity, self-possession, resilience, and grounding. In chapter 4, I describe how we can actually feel the qualities of our intelligence, love, voice, power, and sexuality and so recover these vital aspects of ourselves from the crushing impact of trauma. In the next chapter, I describe how we can access a subtle channel that runs through the vertical core of our torso, neck, and head. Long-known to spiritual practitioners, this subtle core of the body is not only an entranceway into fundamental consciousness, it is also the deepest contact that we can have with our individual being. From the innermost perspective of this channel, we gain both our greatest distance and our oneness with the world around us. We also gain perspective on our own thoughts, emotions, and sensations, not as a dis-ownership of that content of experience but as disentanglement, so we can allow life to flow.

In chapter 6, I describe how trauma affects our senses, limiting and distorting our perception with memories of painful and abrasive sensory experiences. As we release the trauma-based constrictions from our senses, our environment appears more vivid and unified; we feel that we are perceiving our world clearly and directly. Chapter 7 focuses on relationships and on how inhabiting the body, knowing ourselves as fundamental consciousness, and releasing the remnants of relational trauma from our body can help us feel safe to connect with other people. As fundamental consciousness, we can experience deep intimacy with others without losing inward contact with ourselves. We can also see through the trauma-based fears and projections that occur in our relationships so that our traumatic past no longer hinders our openness to love.

Next I present the Realization Process release technique for recognizing and releasing the trauma-based patterns that we have bound in our body. This is a unique and effective technique that applies the refined focus of the more subtle realms of our being to releasing these holding patterns along their exact pathways. This precision, along with the release of emotions that have been held in the constrictions, the uncovering of traumatic memories, the resolution of the faulty beliefs based on those memories, and the embodiment practices of the Realization Process, produces a lasting freedom from our traumatic history. In chapter 9, I describe methods from the Realization Process that facilitate our healing of anxiety and depression. The last chapter focuses on the relationship between healing trauma and spiritual awakening. It discusses some of the misinterpretations of popular spiritual teachings that can contribute to trauma, rather than help you to heal it. Throughout the book, I have included practices from the Realization Process for inhabiting your body, attuning to the essential qualities of your being, knowing yourself as the fundamental ground of consciousness, and perceiving and relating to other people as this ground.

I have also included an appendix that is directed toward psychotherapists and other healers who are interested in working with the Realization Process. The appendix provides a description of how the realization of fundamental consciousness enhances the therapeutic relationship and how the Realization Process practices can supplement the treatment of specific personality patterns.

May this book help you to heal and to uncover the unity within yourself and the oneness of yourself with the world around you.

HOW WE ORGANIZE OURSELVES

And do not forget, even a fist once
was an open palm and fingers.

YEHUDA AMICHAI

From the very beginning of our lives, even from before we are born, we organize ourselves in response to our environment. We pull away, with our body and our consciousness, from whatever is painful or overwhelming, and we constrict those parts of ourselves that are experiencing pain. Our pulling away from abrasive stimuli is not just a mental process. It is an actual constricting against the sensation of pain.

I define trauma as any event that is too intense, too painful—emotionally or physically—or too confusing to be fully received. In severe trauma, such as sexual abuse, people often dissociate from their body entirely, even leaving their body and viewing the violation from above. But in childhood, even small, ordinary events can be traumatic. These ordinary events are sometimes called developmental trauma or relational trauma. A mother's loving face suddenly changing to an angry or sad expression can be traumatic in this way. A loss of a loved person, or even a loved pet, can be too much for a child to digest. This is especially true if mourning is discouraged, for example, by well-meaning adults trying to stay cheerful for the sake of the child. Certainly, being yelled at or being punished, even in a way that seems mild to the parents, can be too humiliating or frightening for a child to absorb. I worked with a woman who was punished as a child by being sent to her room. This punishment, seemingly so much less severe than being spanked or beaten, was remembered by my client thirty years later with dread, shame, and the bleak despair of the outcast, a feeling she had carried within her body all of her life.

We organize ourselves in reaction to trauma through the medium of the fascia, a dimension of fibers that pervade the whole body and that surround every part of the body, no matter how small. And through the fascia, we can contract any part of our body. We can even constrict ourselves within the internal depth of body, where this contraction is difficult (although not impossible) for an observer to detect. For example, we can shut down our capacity to love with just the smallest movement of the fascia within our chest.

Since the fascia is everywhere in our body as an interconnected substance, it is a dimension of our internal wholeness. This means that when we constrict the fascia in one part of our body, it pulls on other parts of the body. This is something like twisting a balloon—even a small torque on one part of the balloon will affect the overall shape. In a human being, there is not just a single twist, but a complexity of constrictions, each producing tension throughout the whole body.

Over time, if the same movements into constriction are repeated, they may become well-worn, unconscious pathways of reaction to any circumstances that resemble the initial traumatic events of our childhood. For example, we may slightly withdraw our head, in a protective, turtlelike movement, whenever we meet someone in authority if that was how we reacted in childhood to a dominating parent. This habitual echo of our childhood keeps us from experiencing authority figures in the present and impedes our ability to perceive them clearly without feeling intimidated or threatened.

Our repetitive movements into constriction in reaction to childhood trauma may also cause the tissues of the fascia to become glued together. They may harden into the constricted shape. In this way, we develop areas of chronic rigidity throughout our body. In other words, that slight turtlelike withdrawal of our head into our neck may gel into a way of holding ourselves that seems permanent.

This may sound like a horror story, but in fact it is simply the ordinary human condition. We all grow up to some extent limited in our human capacities, such as our ability to love, to speak freely, or to think clearly, by these holding patterns in our fascia. Although we may be aware of feelings of tension in our body, most people are generally not aware of the limitations in their ability to receive and respond to life, unless these limitations become severe. Most of us accept our limitations as being "just who we are." But as children, exquisitely attuned and reactive to the responses of other people, particularly our caregivers, as well as to the sensory stimuli in our environment, we have created this shape of who we are. We have each created our unique design of openness and obstruction to stimulation. This organization of ourselves is not usually a conscious or volitional movement. It is a spontaneous, unconscious reaction to our environment.

Our design of openness and constriction determines where we live in ourselves. If we have constricted our pelvis, we will live more in our upper body, and we will experience life more fully in our upper body. Wherever we live in ourselves, we are available for experience and responsive to our environment. If we have constricted our chest, but remained open in our head, we will tend to think more about life than to respond emotionally. Also, wherever we are more open and in contact with ourselves, we are more capable of contact with other people. This will affect all of our relationships and produce the particular satisfactions and obstacles that we experience with intimate partners.

There is a direct correlation between our human capacities and our physical anatomy. We cannot keep ourselves from crying, for example, except by constricting the anatomy involved in crying. We cannot keep ourselves from feeling sexual response, or sexual fear, except by constricting those parts of our body involved in sexual arousal. We cannot keep ourselves from expressing anger except by closing off our throat or from feeling anger except by constricting our gut and other parts of the body involved in that emotion.

You can try this out for yourself. If you have access to your own emotional responsiveness, take a moment to evoke a feeling of anger. Now try to curb that anger, to keep yourself from feeling it, and observe what happens in your body. You can try the same thing with sadness, anxiety, or fear. The body, as the instrument of our experience, is directly involved in the suppressing of experience.

Any part of the body can be constricted in this way. We limit our vision in order to diminish the impact of confusing or painful visual stimuli, such as a parent beating a sibling or a drunken or furious expression on someone we love. A sensitive child may even limit their vision to block out overly bright colors or frightening images in paintings or on television. They may limit their hearing to dampen an abrasive sound, such as angry voices or even the ticking of a clock. These constrictions in our senses, if they become chronically held patterns, will limit our ability to perceive the world in its true vividness. Again, most people do not know that they are experiencing a somewhat dimmed down version of their surroundings; they just assume that this is how things look and sound. It is not until they can release the chronic holding patterns in their senses that the beauty in their environment is revealed to them and perception becomes a source of pleasure.

We even constrict our skin against painful or overly stimulating tactile experiences. Later, as adults, this constriction will limit our ability to experience sensual pleasure, as well as physical pain. I worked with a man who said that he had been regularly whipped by his father with a belt, but that he never felt anything at all during these punishments. He had numbed himself to both the physical pain and the humiliation of being beaten. As he related this to me, he expanded his chest proudly and defiantly—he had not allowed his father to hurt him. I had to look deeply into his eyes to see the anguished, furious, shamed child, wincing in pain, an expression, I realized, that was always there in the background of whatever else he was expressing. But he had to regain contact with those parts of his body that had been abused before he became aware of this pain himself. As we worked together, it became clear that he had managed to tighten even the skin of his buttocks against the shock of his father's belt. After he released this holding pattern, he confided in me that, for the first time, he was taking great pleasure in the feel of his wife's touch on his bare body.

These constrictions serve the vital purpose of keeping ourselves intact, of not losing our central organizing function that keeps track of ourselves and our environment. They allow us to manage our environment so we are not overwhelmed by it and to manage ourselves so we maintain, as much as possible, the love and approval from our caretakers that we need for our survival and development. So although our constrictions diminish us, and even fragment us, they keep us from shattering. They guard against the degree of overwhelm that can cause, in extreme trauma, the disintegration of our sense of self, of our sense of existing as a single, cohesive person over time.

We all grow up to some extent less than we could be: less emotionally responsive, less capable of sexual pleasure, less creative and intelligent. We grow up in a world that has, to some extent, become dulled down by these early organizations of ourselves: less vivid in its colors and sounds and textures. Releasing these constrictions means that we gradually regain both the fullness of our natural capacities and the clarity of the world around us.

Most of the binding in our body occurs in early childhood. But some patterns are formed later in childhood in response to peers and other adults that we encounter. Many grade-school and adolescent boys, for example, organize their bodies to defend against the threat of physical attack from their peers. A man came to work with me several years ago who was a psychotherapist. He embodied many of the best traits of our shared profession. His face was open and sympathetic, his manner gentle but grounded and direct. As I sat with him, I was reminded that many people in our generation, for he was the same age as me, had managed to eradicate at least some of the worst expressions of gender stereotype. For there was none of the clichéd male arrogance or attempt to dominate in this man, none of the bullying posture. He seemed to meet me as an equal, without either exaggerating or diminishing his own strength.

Yet there was part of him that seemed to be somehow at odds with the rest of his demeanor. While he sat comfortably on the couch, his arms appeared to be stuck to his torso, rigid and also energized, as if in readiness for action. He seemed entirely unaware of this mixed message expressed by his body. It turned out that, although he had been through years of therapy and explored his early childhood and his relationship with his parents thoroughly, he had never explored his life as a young adolescent among his peers. He had grown up in a neighborhood marked by poverty and frustration, in which the young males formed fierce loyalties and exacted retribution for any behavior perceived as disloyal. My client was not a fighter. He had tried to focus on his education as a way of escaping the misery he saw around him, spending his time after school in libraries and on his school's debate team. But in order to get to school or to the library, he had to walk down streets filled with young men who were fighters, who might at any time threaten him physically. He learned to organize himself in an attitude of strength, to hold his arms as if in readiness to strike. Now, many years later, and living the most peaceful of lives, his body was still geared for battle.

Adolescents also pattern themselves in order to conform to the stereotypes of male and female sexual attractiveness. Girls especially may organize themselves in order to bring attention to their breasts, behind, or legs. They may also organize themselves to mask these parts of themselves, as a protection against the amount or the type of attention they are suddenly receiving.

In order for the patterns of constriction to become bound in our body, they usually need to be repeated many times over the course of our childhood or adolescence. An exception to this is extreme trauma, such as sexual abuse or a terrible accident, such as a car crash. In catastrophic events, we may defend ourselves with such intensity that a lasting constriction is produced from a single event. We may also retain the memory of the impact of what is done to us in the tissues of our body even after the injury itself has healed. We may retain the memory of the impact of a car accident, for example, or the imprint of the forceps used to induce our birth.

We can also form patterns of constriction as adults. In general, the patterns of constriction that we form as adults are in reaction to extreme trauma. A woman came to work with me with a severe constriction in her abdomen. As she released it, the memories that surfaced for her were of an illness that had occurred about twenty years previously when she was a young woman. She was newly married, and her husband's work took them to a small Middle Eastern country. This woman found herself in a hospital, with a frightening illness, surrounded by strangers speaking a language that she did not understand. After several weeks in the hospital, she received abdominal surgery. During this time, her husband's work kept him away during the days, and she described feeling more alone and more terrified than she had ever felt in her life. The constriction in her abdomen was her reaction to the invasive surgery, as well as to the terror and sense of abandonment that overwhelmed her as she lay in the hospital bed.

All of our holding patterns contain the movement into the constriction and therefore the exact pathway of their release. This brings us back to the analogy of the balloon. If we hold a balloon in a twisted shape and then let go, the balloon will return to its original shape along the same pathway of the twist. Later in the book, I describe the Realization Process release technique, which makes use of this bound pathway, preserved within the tensions of our body.

Why We Constrict

Although we fragment and constrict ourselves unconsciously, without calculation, all of our constrictions serve important purposes. Most of our patterns of constriction are for protection or to help us maintain the love and approval of our caretakers, which we need in order to survive and flourish, by restraining those aspects of ourselves that seem to displease them. But we also organize ourselves for other reasons. We unconsciously mirror the pattern of openness and protection of our caretakers, and later in childhood, of our peers. In this way, we "fit in" with the other members of our family or with our friends, so we can most easily enjoy contact and communication with them.

We also constrict those parts of ourselves that do not receive the stimulation of contact from our caretakers. This is because we actually need the stimulation of contact in order to deepen contact with ourselves, and in those parts of ourselves that are not nurtured in this way, we may shut down. We also form ourselves to conform to the demands and even the unspoken needs of our caretakers, for example, for quiet in the house or for turning a blind eye to family problems, again to maintain our place as a loved and accepted member of the family. We may organize ourselves to embody the way we are seen in our family or the role that we serve in the family dynamic, such as the "good for nothing" one, chronically deflated in a posture of failure, or the kind but comically stupid one, with a bound pattern of constriction in our intelligence. Finally, feeling the limitations of our constrictions, we may form chronic patterns of compensation in our body, for example, puffing out our chest in a simulation of pride or power.

Protection

The most common reason for constricting yourself is to lessen the impact of painful, confusing, or overwhelming stimulation. As you begin to release these organizations in your body, you may discover that the areas in your body of bound fascia contain your child mind (your childhood mentality at the time of trauma), the memory of what happened to you, and the emotions you felt during the trauma.

My evidence for this is experiential. Over the past thirty-five years, I have observed thousands of people experience the emergence of memories, emotions, and childhood mentality as they release the constrictions in their body. I am not alone in this observation. Bodyworkers, such as Structural Integration and craniosacral practitioners, as well as psychotherapists working in body-oriented modalities, have long reported this phenomenon.

Often several memories and ages are held within the same constriction. You use the same movement into constriction to protect against similar painful stimuli at different times in your childhood. For example, if you tighten in your stomach area when you are afraid of your mother's anger as a two-year-old child, you may tighten in the same area when you are afraid of going to school for the first time at age five or in any frightening situation. When you begin to release this part of your body through therapeutic methods as an adult, you may uncover several different memories of being afraid at different times in your early life.

Protecting yourself from your environment involves not just keeping external stimuli out, but also holding in whatever might be hazardous to express. For example, if crying when you are punished brings about an intensification of your parent's anger, then you may learn to hold back your tears. You may also hold back tears that you know will not be met with comfort. If it is dangerous to be conspicuous in your family, you may constrict yourself in order to make yourself appear smaller or less threatening. Or you may dull your own perception of your environment and "space out" in order to pretend to yourself that you are not really there.

Mirroring

You also organize yourself in order to match your parents' pattern of openness and defense. If your parents live mostly in their heads (or foreheads), for example, but are more constricted emotionally, you may also inhabit your head, or forehead, and shut down, to some extent, emotionally. This mirroring, like your protective patterning, is unconscious and spontaneous. Children imitate their parents as whole gestalts. I have often seen a parent walking down the street with a young child by his or her side, who is exactly matching the rhythm and slight imbalance of the parent's gait. As your ability for conversation develops, you match not only vocal accent, tone, and rhythm, but also the placement of your parent in their body as they speak. If your parent lives mostly in their chest while speaking, you may also speak while inhabiting your chest more than other parts of your body. If your parent's voice is constricted, you may match that constriction in your own throat as you learn to speak.

I worked with a man who complained of a constant feeling of tension in his throat. Since most of our sessions were on the phone, I became very sensitive to his voice. I could hear that he did a kind of flattening, a bearing down within his throat whenever he spoke that sounded as if he were squeezing his words out. I also noticed that this bearing down quality in his voice intensified whenever he spoke about his father. He described his father as "witty and sardonic," qualities that he admired except when his father's sharp humor was directed at him. When I asked him to imitate his father's voice, he was able to feel this bearing down within his throat and then to recognize that he did a somewhat milder version of it whenever he spoke. He had taken on his father's way of speaking, unconsciously, as a way of mirroring the father he admired.

Children do not just mirror what they see and hear, but also what they feel in other people. As sensitive children, we do not just relate from the surface of ourselves, but by contacting the internal space of our parents' bodies with the internal space of our own body. In this way, we can mirror constrictions and emotions that are held within the inner depth of our parents' bodies. I remember one woman who went to stay for a few weeks at an ashram in India. She told me that she began to cry as soon as she arrived there and could not stop. After several days, she realized that she was crying because she missed her mother and that she felt both tremendous grief and guilt for abandoning her. Although the emotions were intense, they made no sense to her because her mother was safe at home in Brooklyn. But after a week of heart wrenching sobs, she finally realized that her father had mourned his own mother this intensely after she committed suicide when he was an adolescent. It had been a taboo subject in the family, and she had never heard him speak about it, much less express emotion. But she had carried within her own body the unexpressed grief and guilt that was bound within his body.

This mirroring is a complex process. Most of us have more than one parent, as well as other people, such as grandparents, older siblings or aunts and uncles, and even stepparents or stepsiblings, that we may live with and mirror. What we mirror is influenced by many factors, including the personality that we are born with, our particular gifts, and our specific relationship with each family member. The apparently inborn aspects of our personality with its innate gifts and challenges are a mystery. Theories on personality range from the random throw of genetic dice to less knowable possibilities, such as reincarnation. But whatever the origins are, our pattern of openness and constriction in the fascia can be recognized, and the constrictions can be released.

Here is another illustration of mirroring one's parents' holding patterns. Leslie worried about money incessantly. Although he was now comfortably retired, with money in the bank and a beautiful home, he still found himself feeling afraid each time a new bill arrived or the house needed repairs. He knew that he had been brought up in an atmosphere of fear about money and that his father also worried that he would not be able to support his family. Even though Leslie's father had also made a good living, he and Leslie's mother were always on the lookout for bargains and only shopped at discount stores. Leslie recognized that this family attitude was based on his father's childhood, during the depression, when his father's family were very poor. His father had often gone to school in clothes that he had long outgrown, in pants that were too short, and shirts that had been patched and repatched. The other children had made fun of his father's appearance and of the meager contents of his lunchbox.

Leslie had a chronically deflated chest. Over the course of our work together, we had found a few different causes for this pattern, and it had begun to release. As Leslie spoke about his money fears and his father's money fears, this pattern once again became more pronounced.

It often happens that when a person speaks about their childhood, the holding patterns in their body that correspond with those memories become intensified and easier both for an observer (the therapist) to see and for the person speaking to feel.

Now, as Leslie spoke about his father's fears, I could see his father's constricted chest within Leslie's chest. It had a slightly different feel, more deeply shamed, and somehow more naïve than the mentality of the patterns in Leslie's body that related to his own childhood history. I asked Leslie to picture his father in front of him. "Where does he hold his fears about money in his body?" I asked.

As Leslie imagined his father's body, his hands came up to his upper chest. "Here," he said. "And in his solar plexus." As Leslie experienced his father's money fears in his own body, he also became aware of a deep sense of shame. "This is shame I've always felt, deep down. But I've never known what I was so ashamed about. This is his shame, my father's shame."

This was a pattern that Leslie had mirrored unconsciously at a very young age, along with an inexplicable sense of humiliation and worry about survival. But knowing that this was his father's shame and worry, and not his own, made it easier for Leslie to release it.

Nurture

No matter how open you are at birth, you need the stimulation of connection with another human being in order to deepen your inward connection with yourself and therefore to mature in your capacities for understanding, emotional responsiveness, and physical sensation. Parents nurture and help mature their children through the medium of contact. If the parents inhabit their chests, they are available for emotional contact and will nurture that capacity in their child. If parents inhabit their heads and are available for intellectual contact, they will nurture that capacity in their child. If parents are comfortable and open in their sexuality, the natural, nonsexual, nonintrusive contact between their own pelvis and their child's will help the child deepen contact within their own pelvis so that their own sexuality can continue to mature.

You are likely to constrict those aspects of yourself that are not met and nurtured by parental contact. These parts of yourself are still present, but they exist within their constricted condition. Circumstances later in life, or therapeutic methods, can help open and mature these dormant parts of yourself.

Sometimes relationships, especially intimate relationships with people who are not constricted in the same ways that you are, can help nurture those capacities that did not receive nurture when you were a child. The stimulation of education and art may also contribute to deepening these neglected and constricted aspects of yourself. Sometimes just the suggestion to attune to these shutdown aspects of yourself, such as in the Realization Process embodiment practices, are sufficient to bring them to life. Or they may require the more focused work of releasing these constrictions from the fascia. If your childhood capacity for love was not met with the response of parental love, for example, you may need to do the same focused release work within the constrictions in your chest that we usually need to do with protective holding patterns.

Compliance

You may also organize yourself in response to either spoken or nonverbal cues from your parents and from other significant people in your childhood. If your mother seems to feel sad whenever you feel sad, you may attempt to keep a happy expression on your face, that if chronically held, may rigidify into a static expression that has nothing to do with what you are really feeling. If your mother appears to be burdened by her chores of housework and childcare, you may suppress your own needs so as not to add to her troubles. For example, you may restrain your tears so that she does not have the extra job of comforting you.

Children thrive on approval. They are keenly attuned to the shifting winds of approval and disapproval in their environment. If their intelligence is praised, it will deepen and mature. If their affection is appreciated, that will continue to blossom. But if they are told, "Don't be so smart," they may actually constrict the instrument of their intelligence and abandon, to some extent, the internal space of their head. If they are told repeatedly, and especially angrily, to "quiet down" or to be less active or vital, they can only comply with those commands by holding back their voice or by holding themselves still. I worked with a woman who had been repeatedly told to sit still during the daily family prayers and that any movement would be seen by God and punished. She was in her forties when she finally recognized that she was still wearing the "full body corset" of tension that she had believed God required of her.

Children are also sometimes told that their view of reality is incorrect. Their parents may adamantly insist, for example, that they are not angry or drunk or unhappy as the child perceives them to be. When faced with this parental denial of their perception, they will often accept the parental view, dulling their own vision, hearing, and understanding to accommodate it. Children may be faced with a terrible choice: truth or love. They can limit their own senses and intelligence and be cozily embraced by the family. Or they can stick to their view of reality, shutting down their heart instead of their wits and enduring the family rejection. We often see these two different routes among siblings in the same family, leading to complex family dynamics.

Compensation

As you get older and need to relate with your peers, you may also form holding patterns that compensate for the limitations that you have created in yourself with your protective, compliant, and mirroring patterns. A child who has been overpowered, for example, by a dominating or abusive parent, will often contract their natural sense of power in their body, usually by constricting in the midsection of the torso. When they need to go out into their school environment, and later, their work environment, they may feel easily overpowered by other people. Although this constriction of power is unconscious, they may be aware of feeling somehow less substantial than other people. To counter this, some people will bolster their appearance of strength by lifting upward in their body or jutting forward in their chin or forehead in a typical bullying stance. This compensatory adjustment is generally as unconscious as the original constriction of power. Over time, these compensatory patterns may also become rigidly held within the body.

Conclusion

As we release these organizations in our fascia, we have a greater sense of our internal volume, of taking up space. We gain more of our being, and this means that we actually feel more alive.

All of our constrictions are moments of our past that we have stopped in their tracks and held in that way, unconsciously. They are frozen moments of our past. But what is frozen can unfreeze, can become fluid. When we focus within these rigidities, we can free this movement and then inhabit those parts of our body that have been lost to us. Instead of living partially in the past, we can live more wholly in the present moment.

2

FUNDAMENTAL CONSCIOUSNESS

For the nothingness of Zen is not lifeless like
emptiness, but, on the contrary, is something
quite lively. It is not only lively but also has
heart, and moreover, is aware of itself.

SHIN'ICHI HISAMATSU

I n the Realization Process, recovery from trauma is approached
through releasing the bound organizations from the fascia and
by doing specific practices for inhabiting the internal space of
the body and attuning to the pervasive space of fundamental consciousness. In this method, the practices for inhabiting the body and
realizing oneself as fundamental consciousness precede the work of
releasing holding patterns from the body. This is so we can experience
the safety and stability of our underlying wholeness before releasing
patterns that may have served important protective functions in our
childhood. When we increase our openness to life by releasing the
rigid constrictions in our body, we do not open into nothingness, but
into the underlying, unbreakable, unified ground of our being.

For most people, both inhabiting the body and realizing oneself as
fundamental consciousness are new experiences. In this chapter, I will

describe the experience of fundamental consciousness. Since it is actually easier to experience than to imagine or understand conceptually, I will also provide, in the next chapter, the main Realization Process practice for uncovering and knowing ourselves as this ground of our being.

Since we have not yet been able to find a conclusive scientific explanation for fundamental consciousness, I cannot say with any certainty, in terms that would satisfy us in the twenty-first century, what this experience actually is. But I do know that we can experience it, and that when we do, it benefits us profoundly.

Fundamental consciousness is experienced as an underlying stillness, but a palpable, lively stillness, pervading our body and our environment at the same time. When we know ourselves as this pervasive stillness, everything—all of the "content" of our experience—appears to emerge out of this stillness with extraordinary clarity as if, for the first time, we are seeing things as they really are.

Another way of saying this is that as fundamental consciousness (FC), we perceive life with less subjective distortion. Since FC is our own consciousness, it is a dimension of our own subjectivity. It is now understood by most of science and philosophy that we can never have an entirely objective view of reality. The observed is always to some extent interpreted and changed by the observer. The world we live in is always a world that we have learned to perceive and understand in specific ways based on our personal and cultural background.

However, our subjectivity can be more or less distorted. We can live almost entirely in our own world, thickly coloring everything we see with our imagination and with our desires, fears, and aversions. Or we can become increasingly open to the world around us and increasingly attuned to FC as the ground level of our experience. The twentieth-century Zen philosopher Nishitani called this ground of consciousness the "near side" of subjectivity.[1] It is a subjective experience of life, but relatively free from fantasy. We feel that we have become more real and that our perception of our environment has become more true. When we are attuned to this basis of authenticity, we become better equipped to distinguish authenticity from falsehood in ourselves and in the world around us, such as in the demeanor and vocal tone of other people.

Fundamental consciousness is a dimension of disentanglement, of non-grasping. All of life's movements flow through the stillness of this ground, without obstruction. When we know ourselves as FC, we are able to allow the free flow and therefore the full impact, or full intensity, of our emotions, sensations, thoughts, and perceptions without clamping down on them. This means fundamental consciousness is the basis of our most direct, unfiltered contact with life. When we touch, we really feel what we are touching; when we look, we see the object of our focus vividly. When we feel sad, it is a deep movement within our body. When we are inspired, we experience our creativity clearly and fluidly.

The experience of fundamental consciousness is not of something separate from ourselves. Although we experience fundamental consciousness, it is more correct to say that it experiences itself. We do not know it as an object, separate from our own being, for we experience that it is our own being. Fundamental consciousness is self-knowing. It is realized when our consciousness becomes conscious of itself. It requires, and is, a refinement of our own consciousness.

It is not widely known that our consciousness is capable of refinement. If we look at a tree, for example, we may see only our preconceived idea of a tree. Or we may see just its shape and color and texture. Or we may, looking at this same tree, perceive the subtle spaciousness pervading it and the movement of life force within it.

With this more sensitive attunement, the world we live in is not exactly the same as the world we lived in before this refinement. It is more vivid, nuanced, and even luminous. But it is still the world. When we perceive the tree in this more subtle way, it is still the actual tree. To know ourselves as the subtle ground of our being is a distinct shift from fragmentation to wholeness, but it is who we actually are. Rather than feeling ethereal or supernatural, the experience of fundamental consciousness feels authentic and familiar. Rather than transporting us into another world, it shows us the spacious, unified underpinning of this world. When we experience that we are made of the same one consciousness as everything and everyone that we encounter, it is easier to feel that we belong here, just where we are.

Although I describe fundamental consciousness as pervading our body and environment, the word "pervade" can be misleading. "Pervade" is a verb, and fundamental consciousness does not move. It is experienced as a pervasive stillness. Objects within this pervasive space appear to be permeable. They appear to be made of empty, luminous space, at the same time as they appear to be material and solid. This is not physical space, not the space within which subatomic particles are spinning. It is the space of consciousness. Fundamental consciousness is experienced as extending everywhere in space, not just around, but through all of the objects within this space.

This permeability of our environment takes some practice to experience, and it is difficult to describe in words. It is an actual sensory experience, but it requires the refinement and unification of the senses that occur as we realize fundamental consciousness in order to experience it. We do see the permeability of objects, but we do not actually see through objects—we cannot, for example, see what is behind a wall. Yet we experience, we "see-feel" that our consciousness does permeate right through the wall at the same time as it permeates our own body. Interestingly, if we attempt to experience this permeability without embodying fundamental consciousness, we cannot do it. Fundamental consciousness is a mutual permeability of self and other.

When people struggle to experience this, I suggest that they just spend a few moments each day sitting in front of any object, attuning to the space pervading their own body and the object, until this permeability of self and object emerges. Sometimes, students who have practiced the Realization Process for some time, months or even years, will suddenly announce, as if they have just been humoring me all this time, "Everything is really pervaded by space!"

Fundamental consciousness is vitally important for healing from trauma because it cannot be injured. It has never been injured, no matter how severe our traumatic experiences have been. When we realize ourselves as FC, we know that we have not been irreparably damaged. We can actually feel that who we really are, who we have always, deep down, known that we are, has always been there, intact. This fundamental ground of ourselves, the "near side of our subjectivity" has been there to witness our shattered, traumatized state, without being shattered itself. We are basically whole, and that underlying wholeness cannot be fragmented or diminished. Only our access to our wholeness has been obstructed.

Also, because life flows through this pervasive space without changing it (without changing us at this fundamental level of our identity), we gain greater resilience to both sensory stimuli and our internal responses. We can receive the full intensity of life without feeling shattered or overwhelmed.

While trauma fragments us, the realization of ourselves as fundamental consciousness unifies our body, heart, and mind. We created all of our holding patterns in reaction to our environment. These holding patterns do not only produce fragmentations within our body, but also between ourselves and our environment. Fundamental consciousness is an experience of oneness with our environment and with other people. As this subtle, pervasive dimension of consciousness, it becomes much easier for us to let go of these fragmentations. We find that as FC, we can be open to and connected with other people without our old fears and aversions triggering our patterns of protection. We can remain connected to our internal experience, our own needs and desires, without feeling overwhelmed or annihilated by the presence of other people.

The Qualities of Fundamental Consciousness

When we attune to ourselves as fundamental consciousness, we find that this pervasive space is not empty in the sense of void. Even though it is experienced as stillness, it is lively, luminous stillness.

In the Realization Process, I attempt to avoid metaphysical assertions about what fundamental consciousness actually is or what qualities it actually possesses. However, an important part of the Realization Process, for both healing from trauma and for spiritual awakening, is to attune to specific qualities that appear to be inherent in this lively pervasive space. These qualities, which we can attune to pervading everywhere, are experienced as the fundamental qualities of our own being. In this work, we name these qualities: awareness, emotion, and physical sensation. Attuning to these three qualities can help us feel whole within ourselves and unified with our surroundings.

These three qualities are not specific awarenesses, emotions, and physical sensations. The qualities of the ground are more subtle than the changing content of specific experiences. They do not arise and dissipate like specific experiences. Instead, they are experienced as aspects of the unchanging stillness within which specific perceptions, cognitions, emotions, and physical sensations move.

Before we go further, by "quality," I mean the "feel" of our experience. A distinguishing characteristic of a quality is that it cannot be translated into a direct description of the experience. For example, the quality of love, exactly how it feels, cannot really be conveyed to someone who has not experienced it. We can talk about the experience—we can say that love is warm or that it causes us to want to connect with someone that we feel this toward, but we cannot put into words the exact experience of love itself. In the same way, we cannot convey, to someone who has not experienced it, the color red, the taste of vanilla, or the sensation of coldness. This is true for all of the many qualities that make up our experience, including the unchanging qualities of fundamental consciousness.

I divide the qualities of fundamental consciousness into these three categories because we attune to each quality through a different section of our body. We attune to the ground of awareness in, around, and above our head. By awareness, I mean that part of the ground within which perceptions and thoughts occur. We attune to the ground of emotion in the mid-third of our body—our chest and mid-section. By emotion, I mean that part of the ground within which emotions, such as grief, anger, and joy, occur. We attune to physical sensation through the bottom third of our body—our lower torso, legs, and feet. By physical sensation, I mean that part of the ground in which physical sensations, such as heat and sexual pleasure occur.

Although I divide the qualities of FC into these three categories, they are experienced as a spectrum of qualities in our body, rather than as clearly divided aspects of ourselves. And even though we attune to each part of this spectrum through different sections of our body, all of the qualities are experienced pervading everywhere in our body and in our environment. This means that we experience the ground of fundamental consciousness as a blend of awareness, emotion, and physical sensation. Although this is difficult to grasp intellectually, it is not difficult to experience, as you may discover if you do the practice of attuning to the qualities of fundamental consciousness in chapter 4.

If we do not attune to all three qualities of fundamental consciousness, we will have only a partial contact with ourselves and a partial openness to life. And because fundamental consciousness is a unified ground, a partial realization is not yet the subtle, pervasive space of fundamental consciousness. It is not yet the most basic, unified ground of our being.

In many spiritual teachings, the fundamental ground is referred to as "awareness." I believe that this term is misleading. It can cause spiritual practitioners to open to it just in their head or even just around their head. But the ground of our being pervades and is opened to throughout our whole being. That is why, in the Realization Process, we name and experience these qualities as awareness, emotion, and physical sensation.

Our design of constriction and openness determines where we live in ourselves. It can also determine what we cultivate in meditation. Meditation practitioners tend to dwell, during their meditation, in the parts of their body that they are most accustomed to and where they are already most open. So someone who lives mostly within their head will dwell within their head while they meditate. In this way, they will become increasingly open in this part of themselves as they continue to meditate. But the rest of their body will not become more open and may never become open enough to reach the fundamental dimension of consciousness.

Likewise, someone who lives primarily in the emotional aspect of themselves will dwell within their chest during meditation and become increasingly open emotionally without opening the rest of their body to fundamental consciousness. Some meditation techniques emphasize one aspect of our being more than others (such as awareness or love), and practitioners of those methods may also become increasingly imbalanced.

Opening to all three qualities of fundamental consciousness is important for psychological health because it brings balance and fullness to our ordinary life experience. Someone who dwells mostly in their head or the space around their head may be cognitively adept but cut off from their emotional and sensual experience. But without the emotional and sensual aspects of consciousness, even our understanding and our abstract reasoning will be limited because it will not be fully informed by our life experience.

Or, if a person lives mostly in their chest, their emotional experience may become overwhelming because it is not balanced by the capacity to reason or the grounding of physical sensation. They may feel tuned in to the emotional pain of the people around them without the understanding necessary to encompass that pain or to see a way to overcome it. Their emotional responses may become so intense that they eventually attempt to shut down their emotional capacity or to avoid emotionally charged situations.

Someone who lives mostly in their lower body may become so engrossed in physical sensation that they become ruled by their love of sensual pleasure, without feeling what would nourish them emotionally and without recognizing the possible negative outcomes of following all of their sensual desires.

We need to be attuned to all three qualities of fundamental consciousness in order to reach our most subtle and most complete experience of ourselves and the world around us. The blend of awareness, emotion, and physical sensation pervading everywhere helps us attune to and resonate with the awareness, emotion, and physical sensation in other people and in all of nature. Sometimes people ask me if this means that even the inanimate objects that we experience as pervaded by fundamental consciousness are conscious themselves. Whether the chair or the table have awareness, emotion, and physical sensation. My answer to this is no. Even though we can experience these objects as pervaded by quality-rich consciousness, inanimate objects themselves, as far as I know, are not conscious.

Consciousness is distributed on a spectrum among forms in nature. Some forms are more conscious than others. Even if fundamental consciousness is the actual underlying nature of the universe, as some Asian teachings (for example, Advaita Vedanta) claim, the consciousness of each specific form would be determined by its degree of openness to this ground.

A being needs to have some degree of consciousness before we can experience mutual contact with them, before they can meet our consciousness with their own. Although a sensitive person can have some sense of mutual communion with a tree, there is more potential for mutual contact with a dog, for example, and still more with a human being.

It takes a high degree of consciousness for us to become attuned to and aligned with fundamental, pervasive consciousness—for consciousness to become conscious of itself. According to Buddhist teachings, only human beings are capable of realizing their fundamental nature. Some people would argue, though, that they have met and even swam with enlightened creatures of other species.

3

INHABITING THE BODY

I've been reading about this stuff for years, but I never
thought I would be able to experience it, and now I can.

A REALIZATION PROCESS STUDENT

I n the Realization Process, we discover the ground of fundamental consciousness by inhabiting the internal space of our body.
Fundamental consciousness is unified—it pervades our body and
environment at the same time. If it did not pervade our body as well
as our environment, it would not be an experience of oneness. For this
reason, we cannot actually realize fundamental consciousness without
also inhabiting the internal space of our body.

Inhabiting the body is not the same as being aware of the body. It is
not a "top-down" experience. Inhabiting the body means that we live
within our body, that we are present throughout the whole internal
space of our body. It means that we feel that we are made of consciousness everywhere in our body.

Inhabiting the body takes practice because, for most of us, we are
changing a life-long habit of not inhabiting our body. Most of us
grow up living in front of our body, and very often above our body as
well. The protective constrictions and other rigid organizations in our
fascia obstruct our inward contact with our body. We are also used to
coming forward in order to connect with other people, even though,

as I will explain in the chapter on relationships, this actually dilutes our connection with others. As children, we may develop patterns of living outside of our body if we need to be hypervigilant to a dangerous or unpredictable environment or just as a way to concentrate more intently on whatever is in front of us. We may live outside of our body because it felt to us, as children, that we would be less conspicuous, and therefore in less danger from abusive people in our environment, if we were less in contact with ourselves. Just as young children may cover their own eyes in order to hide, one of the ways we protect ourselves from others is by hiding from ourselves.

One woman told me that when her father came home drunk at night, he would get all five children out of bed, line them up in the living room, and then select one for the focus of his rage. She found that if she left her body, he was less likely to choose her. She felt that she could make herself invisible by diffusing herself outward so that she had a sense of dissolving in the space around her body. Over time, this pattern of outward diffusion became chronic and unconscious. When I met her, she was still holding herself in this pattern of self-abandonment, although it had been many years since she was in danger of her father's violence.

If it felt safer in childhood not to be present within one's body, then coming back into the body can feel frightening. It can also feel taboo, as if we are breaking a rule that we have lived under all our lives, a law against existing as individuals. When we live within our own skin, we become separate from other people, even as we enter into the dimension of oneness with them. I have worked with many people who looked to me for permission to inhabit their own body. They needed support to counter their old agreement with their parents that they would never separate from them.

When we inhabit the body as fundamental consciousness, the constructed, protective boundary between inner and outer experience naturally dissolves. It is transcended, or traversed, by the unified, pervasive ground of FC. This means that we can experience the internal space of our body as continuous with the space pervading our environment. If we inhabit our chest, for example, then we experience the present moment occurring inside and outside of our chest at the same time. This is not a matter of divided attention. Fundamental consciousness is more subtle than our focus of attention. Our focus of attention can shift, but fundamental consciousness does not shift; it is experienced as stillness, pervading inside our body and outside of our body at the same time. You can try this out for yourself.

Take a moment to inhabit the internal space of your chest.

Fill your chest with yourself, with your own being. See if you can feel that you are living within your whole chest, all the way through to your upper back, and out to the sides of your chest.

You may be able to feel that by inhabiting your chest, you can experience this present moment inside and outside of your chest as a unity. In other words, you may be able to experience your surroundings at the same time as you experience whatever emotions or thoughts you are having as you do that.

Wherever you are in contact with the internal space of your body, you are open, permeable, and responsive to your environment. By inhabiting your chest, you will experience deeper, more fluid emotional responsiveness to your environment.

Wherever you live in your body, you are also present within your body. You will have a felt sense, which can also be sensed by others, of being present. Inward contact with yourself, openness to your environment, and presence all occur in the same way, by inhabiting your body.

To be present, open, and conscious everywhere in our body means that you have access to all of your being at once. You receive life with your whole being and respond with your whole being. You can sense, feel, know, and perceive at the same time. When you touch a leaf, for example, this is not just a tactile experience. Your experience of the leaf is sensual, emotional, and cognitive simultaneously. Although the content of your experience, at any given moment, may register more in one realm of yourself than another, all of your modalities of experience are engaged in each moment.

It is not often recognized in conventional psychotherapy that there is an underlying wholeness, or a potential for wholeness, that we can access as we let go of our patterns of fragmentation. For example, the psychoanalyst Elizabeth Howell speaks of the fragmentations that result from trauma as "ego states" and claims that psychological health is the ability to flow smoothly between our various ego states.[1]

But in the Realization Process, we recognize that we can experience a ground of our being that is more subtle than these constructed ego states. It feels naturally unified and naturally existent. Fundamental consciousness is not something we construct—it is a given, like our physical anatomy. Once we uncover it, we do not shift into different fragments of ourselves in different situations. Although we certainly behave differently and have different emotional responses, we feel like the same person, like who we really are, in every circumstance. From the vantage point of this underlying ground of our being, we can observe the shifts that occur in us as we move through different environments. We can see how we may become humble in relation to one person or feel superior to someone else. With this capacity for observation, we can understand ourselves better and even make changes in our behavior and relationships.

Inhabiting the Body and Attuning to Fundamental Consciousness

There will be parts of ourselves that we cannot inhabit just by changing the habit of disembodiment. Those are areas of ourselves that we have constricted so tightly for so long that the connective tissues of the body (the fascia) have become glued together. These constrictions are often unconscious, split off from our conscious experience of ourselves. Or they may be experienced as chronic tension and pain. We may feel that we are inhabiting our body as a whole, but these deeply held, unconscious constrictions will not be included in our experience of wholeness. These bound parts of ourselves need to be worked with directly through the release technique that I will describe in chapter 8.

We can, however, through the practice of inhabiting the body, release less tightly held constrictions in the body and enter into those parts of ourselves with which we have lost contact. We can also change the habitual placement of ourselves outside of our body with the ability to live within our body.

Many body-oriented therapies cultivate body awareness. However, to inhabit the body is different than being aware of the body. We can be aware of our feet on the floor or our breath filling and emptying our lungs. We can be aware of tension in our neck, pain, or hunger in our belly. To be aware of our body in this way is much better than not being aware of our body. But it is not the same as living within the body. In order to experience the difference, you can try this:

PRACTICE Inhabiting Your Hands

Rest your hands, palms down, on your legs.

Now take a few moments to become aware of your hands.

In becoming aware of your hands, you may feel how tense or relaxed they are. You may feel the temperature of your hands, whether they are cool or warm. This is becoming aware of your hands.

Now enter into your hands. Become present within the internal space of your hands. Let yourself feel that you *are* the internal space of your hands; this is part of who you are. This is inhabiting your hands.

I remember one man's response to this exercise when I first taught it to him. "This is going to sound strange," he said to me. "But it feels as if my hands fit inside my hands. I've never felt that before."

The following is the main practice of the Realization Process. In this practice, you inhabit your whole body, in the same way as you may have felt in the exercise above, by feeling that you live within the internal space of your body. Most people will find some parts of their body easier to inhabit than other parts. That is because of our particular design of constriction and openness—the way we organized ourselves in childhood in relation to our parents and environment.

This practice can facilitate your realization of fundamental consciousness, but it is not the realization itself. The realization of fundamental consciousness is effortless; it requires no volition or intention to maintain it. For this reason, some spiritual teachers say that you should not do any practice. They claim that since this is our true nature, we just need to relax and "settle into it." However, the realization of fundamental consciousness is not simply a relaxed state. In order to settle in to the subtle, unified ground of FC, we need to let go of ourselves from deep within our body. The Realization Process practices cultivate the ability to contact ourselves and open ourselves within the whole internal space of the body so the actual realization of fundamental consciousness can occur. The practices do require effort and concentration, but they lead to the effortlessness of the ground of our being.

PRACTICE Attunement to Fundamental Consciousness

Sit upright. Close your eyes. Focus on your breathing. Silently count two counts to inhale and two counts to exhale. Let your breath be smooth and calm.

Now bring your attention to your feet. Enter into your feet so that you inhabit them. Experience yourself living within your feet. Make sure you can stay in your feet as you continue to breathe, that your inhale does not lift you up away from your feet.

Feel that you are inside your ankles and your lower legs, all the way back to your calves. Take a moment to experience yourself living inside your ankles and calves.

Inhabit your knees. Gently settle down into your knees so that they feel soft inside. Balance your awareness of the space inside both knees—find the inside of both knees at the same time. Let yourself feel the stillness of the balanced mind.

Inhabit your thighs, all the way through to the backs of your thighs. Let yourself experience living inside your thighs.

Feel that you are inside your hip sockets. If you inhabit your hip sockets deeply, you will feel a tiny resonance or vibration within them. Balance your awareness of the space inside both hip sockets—find them both at the same time. Let yourself feel the stillness of the balanced mind and the movement of your breath at the same time.

From the inside of your hip sockets, you can feel the internal space of your upper thighs and the internal space of your lower torso at the same time. You are living within the transition between your legs and your torso.

Inhabit your pelvis. Fill your whole pelvis with yourself. Let yourself settle in your pelvis so that you feel comfortable, living inside your pelvis. This is your foundation. When you inhabit your pelvis, because you have this foundation, your emotional life can settle and rest, and your mental life can settle and rest. Let yourself experience what it feels like to inhabit your pelvis.

Inhabit your midsection, between your ribs and your pelvis. Be sure to inhabit this whole area. Include the solar plexus area under your ribs. Let that soften and inhabit it along with the rest of your midsection. Take a moment to experience yourself living inside your midsection.

Inhabit your chest. Inhabit your chest all the way through to your upper back and out to the sides. Let yourself settle within your chest so that it feels like you are sitting in your heart. Take a moment to experience yourself living within your chest.

Feel that you are inside your shoulders, until they feel soft at the edges.

Inhabit your shoulder sockets. If you inhabit your shoulder sockets deeply, you will feel a slight resonance, or vibration, within them. Balance your awareness of the space inside both shoulder sockets. Find them both at the same time. Let yourself feel the stillness of the balanced mind and the movement of your breath passing through this stillness, without changing it in any way. From inside your shoulder sockets, feel the internal space of your upper arms and your upper torso at the same time. Live in the transition between your arms and your torso, inside your body. Let yourself experience living inside your shoulders and shoulder sockets.

Inhabit your arms, wrists, and hands, all the way to your fingertips. Let yourself feel that they are your arms, your hands. Take a moment to experience yourself living inside your arms, wrists, and hands.

Feel that you are inside your neck. Let yourself gently settle within the cylinder of your neck. Experience yourself living within your neck.

Inhabit your forehead, all the way around to the sides of the forehead. Let your forehead be soft and relaxed. Inhabit your closed eyes. Let your eyes soften so that they feel continuous with the rest of your face. See if you can rest your eyes without floating off into sleep. So that you are relaxed but present within your closed eyes.

Feel that you are behind your cheekbones and inside your nose, all the way to the tip of your nose. Feel that you are inside your jaw, mouth, lips, and chin. Inhabit your ears, not too high up in your ears, but right through the centers of your ears. Take a moment to inhabit your whole face and experience yourself living within your whole face.

Inhabit your brain—not just the front of your brain, but your whole brain, including the bottom, sides, and top of your brain. Let yourself experience living inside your whole brain.

Now inhabit your whole body at once. If we say that the body is the temple, then you are living inside the temple, with nothing left out. Even your toes and fingers and nose are inside the temple. This means that you are making contact with yourself, everywhere in your body at once. Sit for a moment, experiencing yourself living within your whole body, and breathing.

Let yourself experience how you take up space, living within your body. Let yourself experience your aliveness in your whole body. See if you can feel comfortable and at home within your body.

Keeping your eyes closed, find the space outside of your body, the space in the room. This space is above and below you, in front and behind, and on both sides of your body.

Now feel that the space inside your body and outside of your body is the same, continuous space. You are inside your body, but you are permeable—you are pervaded by space. If this is easy for you to feel, let yourself experience that you *are* the space.

Slowly open your eyes. With your eyes open, feel that you are inside your whole body. Even though the world appears, you still have the same temple of your body to sit inside. You may be able to experience the same sense of internal depth with your eyes open that you felt with your eyes closed.

Find the space outside your body. Feel that the space inside and outside of your body is the same, continuous space. You are still inside your body, but you are permeable, pervaded by space.

Without moving at all from within your body, let yourself experience that the space that pervades your whole body also pervades everything in your room. Do not leave your body to find the objects. Rather, find the space that seems to already be there pervading you and all of the objects in the room.

This practice can be used to help you cultivate a sense of safety, self-acceptance, self-love, peacefulness, or any other quality that you feel you need. To do this, just add the quality to each instruction. For example, "Feel that you are in your feet, let yourself feel safe within your feet." Or "Feel that you are in your feet. Take a moment to feel love for yourself within your feet."

If it is challenging for you to attune to the pervasive space, then just do the first part of the practice: inhabiting your body. Wait until you can experience a clear sense of internal volume and of being present within your body before you go on to find the space outside your body and the space that pervades you and your whole environment.

People sometimes experience trembling when they begin to inhabit their bodies. This is the result of long-held tensions releasing. If this occurs, allow it to happen, but then see if you can settle more deeply within your body, into the stillness. Some people feel achiness, as their old tensions finally relax, just as our hand would ache if we opened it after holding it in a fist for several decades. This sensation will soon dissipate. Although it does not happen often, some people feel nausea, the result of all the sickening events that they have endured, while holding back and swallowing their responses. This feeling will also dissipate as you continue to inhabit your body. It may also take some time for us to get used to the feeling of our own aliveness. One woman was terrified that if she felt alive, she would overpower me, that I would disintegrate before her vitality. She kept asking me, "Are you okay?" I had to reassure her, again and again, that I welcomed her aliveness. And that she would not be alone. That I, and many other people, would be able to meet her aliveness with my own. For most people, though, inhabiting the body is a great relief. It feels like coming home, like being born.

The Gifts of Inhabiting Your Own Body

By inhabiting your body, you can recover the internal sources of strength and enjoyment that the traumas in your life have injured. You can gain the expression and feel of your own presence so that you are not intimidated by the presence of others. You can feel safe to be open to life, to be receptive. You can take back the power of agency that may have been lost when you were overpowered by other people or by devastating events. You can become resilient to abrasive sensory stimuli and painful interactions with other people. You can feel grounded, rooted to the earth, so you are not easily unsettled. You can even feel appreciation and compassion for yourself so the responses of your heart and the insights of your own mind are pleasurable.

Becoming Present and Receptive

As fundamental consciousness, we are able to experience our body as made of empty space, as if we were an empty vessel. We are open to life in the same way that a window can be open, rather than shut. We are pure receptivity. However, we can also experience this same internal unified ground as presence—a palpable sense of aliveness, of our own existence. Having an experience of our internal volume, we feel that we take up space. We know ourselves as a living presence in the world.

This tangible sense of existing can help heal the fragility that we often feel as a result of trauma. It gives us the ability to feel that our own existence has equal "weight" or equal potency to the existence of other people so that we do not feel displaced or overpowered by them. People who have been traumatized, as well as people who are naturally very sensitive to the environment, may feel that they can be shattered by external stimuli. But this sense of an internal unified ground cannot be broken. It stands up to the world without our having to exert effort or force.

As presence, we can feel that we are made of innate qualities of being. By innate, I mean unconstructed. We do not have to learn these qualities; we uncover them. The more inward contact we have with our body, the more richly we experience each of these qualities.

Each part of the internal space of our body has a palpable, distinctive quality. We can feel the quality of our intelligence when we inhabit our head. We can experience the quality of our love in our chest, even when we are not actively loving someone or something. We can feel the quality of sexuality and gender within our pelvis. Our personal strength or power has a quality that naturally arises as we inhabit our midsection. And we can even experience the quality of our voice, our potential to speak, when we inhabit our throat.

The emergence of these qualities as we inhabit our body is a potent element of our experience of aliveness. It is also a major aspect of our recovery from trauma. For it is these qualities of ourselves that we diminish in reaction to trauma. If we are overpowered, for example, we may shut down the felt experience of our own power. If we are unloved, abandoned, or rejected, we may shut down our ability to feel love. We constrict these qualities of our being by tightening the parts of our body that are associated with those qualities. Thus, for example, we limit our power by constricting our midsection. We limit our emotional capacity and our ability to feel love by constricting our chest.

As emptiness, we can experience that there is no demarcation at all between ourselves and the space that pervades our whole environment. We experience ourselves as clear-through empty space. But as presence, we can also experience ourselves as possessing permeable but clear boundaries between ourselves and our environment. Inhabiting our body as a whole produces a felt sense of ourselves as a complete form, distinct from other forms. This means that we are able to feel separate from the world around us and still be open and responsive. As this separate, internally unified form, we experience our individuality, and our ownership of our thoughts, feelings, sensations, and perceptions. We experience self-possession. It is this sense of individual ownership, this right to be separate and distinct from others, that is damaged in abusive relationships. When we live within our own body, we regain our access to our own unique experience. We take ourselves back, in a sense, from all of the threats to our safety, the intrusions to our privacy, and the shattering effect of the abrasive stimuli and violence that we endured in the traumatic events of our lives.

Regaining Agency

By inhabiting the body, we can experience our own agency. Agency, the ability to know what we want to do and then do it, is an innate aspect of ourselves that we often lose when we are overpowered. It is almost always part of the outcome of severe trauma, such as sexual abuse or other violence. We can also be overpowered in a slow, chronic way, by being told repeatedly that our own perception and understanding is not accurate or simply does not matter. We can be overpowered by not being heard or by not being valued. Whether the trauma is severe or mild and chronic, the result may be the same. We lose our ability to experience the feeling of wanting something, to know what it is that we want, and then to go toward it.

The loss of agency from trauma also sometimes stems from a sense of having failed oneself, of having "allowed" a terrible thing to happen to oneself. Children almost always feel responsible for the harm done to them. They feel guilty about having been abused. Many theories have been put forth to explain this prevalent phenomenon—the guilt of the victim. Whatever the reason, the self-blame that may occur with trauma may also rob us of our trust in ourselves. We may grow up feeling that we cannot rely on ourselves to guide our own lives effectively. We fear that we may make the wrong decision with disastrous results.

A woman named Jenna came to work with me a few years ago who was always worried about making the wrong decision. She was particularly concerned that her desires might not be aligned with the will of God. "How do I know what is right?" she asked. "How do I know what I am supposed to do?" She had several psychics that she called upon whenever she had to make a decision, such as when to travel or whom to go out with, and even to answer smaller questions, such as what she should be reading or eating. These psychics not only directed her life, they also served as a kind of permission for her to act. Without them, she felt almost paralyzed. But as she began to feel whole within her body, she became less dependent on their guidance. One day she came to the session very excited. "I had the most amazing experience," she said. "I was trying to decide where to go for my summer vacation. I had five options. When I thought of one of them, I felt a strong pull toward it.

I actually felt this pull inside my body. And when I thought of another option, I actually felt a kind of repulsion. And when I thought of the other three, I also felt either this pull toward, or this repulsion, but with less intensity. So I chose the one I felt most pulled toward!"

She had made contact with the innate sense of attraction and repulsion that helps us navigate our lives. If our function of agency is undamaged, we will probably not be aware of this push-pull in our decision-making. We simply go toward what we want. But if we regain it after having lost it, we can sometimes feel it, as Jenna did, as a movement within our body. Some people might question this; for example, what if they are attracted to doing something that is inappropriate, that would be harmful to themselves or others. But when we inhabit our body as whole, this sense of inner guidance also functions as a whole. We do not just follow our emotions, our physical impulses, or our intellectual choices—we are guided by the integration of all of our faculties together.

Restoring Resilience

Inhabiting the body is also important for healing from trauma because it makes us more resilient to external stimulation, such as abrasive sounds or other people's intense emotions. Instead of feeling that sensory or emotional stimuli impinge on us sharply, we have an internal depth in which to receive and absorb the stimulation. The ground of our being, as I have said, cannot be broken. The sounds and sights and the emotional vibrations of other people pass through this unbreakable ground without shattering or displacing us. Even as our reception of life becomes more vivid and more deeply experienced, we remain present and intact. Gaining resilience also means that we are able to more easily recover from the impact of abrasive sensory events or from painful interactions with other people.

I worked with a couple who came to me at the insistence of the wife, Mary, who had a very specific complaint about her husband, Tom. "He won't fight with me," she said. "If I get angry, even a little angry at some small thing, he just clams up. It's like getting angry at a brick wall." She turned to her husband, "And then I get angrier, don't I? I might not have been yelling before, but when you don't respond at all, when you don't even look like you've heard me, then I do start yelling. Don't I?" Tom looked at the floor and nodded his head wordlessly. She turned back to me, "You see?" Tom had closed himself up and ducked his head, as if he were being physically battered.

For several sessions, we addressed Tom's fear of anger and Mary's fear of not being heard that affected the way she expressed her annoyance. It turned out that Tom had been yelled at a lot as a child by a chronically furious mother and that he had learned, very early, to shield himself from her and to tune out the sound of her voice at the first sign of her anger. When I asked him what he felt might happen if he allowed himself to hear his wife's anger, he thought for a moment, and then said, "I feel like I will completely crack open. Like her voice will go right through me and destroy me."

For the next few months, I focused on teaching them the main Realization Process practice of inhabiting the body and attuning to fundamental consciousness. For this couple, it was most important that Tom was able to tolerate the sound of his wife's voice when she was angry so he could respond to her and they could resolve their conflicts.

For some people, it can take some time, even a year or two, before they can experience themselves as the pervasive space of fundamental consciousness, and then still more time for them to be able to stabilize there, to sustain that realization all the time. But many people, like Tom and Mary, are able to realize FC within just a few months of practice.

When Tom was able to experience himself as fundamental consciousness, I asked him to inhabit his body and attune to FC pervading himself and Mary at the same time. Then, as Mary spoke to him, I asked him to receive Mary's voice but allow it to move through the space of FC and through his body, while remaining present within his body. He was able to do this as long as she kept her voice very gentle. But then Mary took the opportunity to voice a complaint about the way he often forgets to take out the garbage early enough on Monday mornings in time for it to be collected. Tom closed up against the sound of her annoyed voice. "Try it again," I said to them. Mary again voiced her complaint, sounding a little more annoyed than she had the first time. Tom was able to remain open this time and to allow the sound of her voice to pass in and through him. Both Mary and I noticed the little spurt of anger that Tom felt as he received Mary's voice. "That was good," I said. "But I got pissed off," Tom said. "Yes," I answered. "If you can allow yourself to receive Mary's anger, you will be able to feel your response to it, and then you can argue about it, or apologize, maybe even fight about it, and then resolve it. If you can remain open in this way, as fundamental consciousness, you will be able feel Mary's anger and whatever you feel in response without either shutting down or falling apart. Neither Mary's anger nor your own can damage this ground of your being."

As fundamental consciousness, we are not detached from experience, we are disentangled from it. This is a big difference. We still feel both what comes through us from our environment and our own response to it. But we allow the movement of both our reception and response to occur and then to dissipate naturally, rather than either obstructing it or holding on to it.

Developing Self-Love

Inhabiting our body is also the basis of self-confidence and even self-love. Most people grow up with a degree of insecurity about themselves. So much is expected of us as children. We face so many tests of memory in school and so many challenging social situations that there is no avoiding a certain amount of failure. If, in addition to these stresses, there is excessive criticism or any other sort of abuse from the adults in our lives, this insecurity may shift into shame and self-loathing. A particularly sensitive child can feel self-doubt or self-hatred even in the face of ordinary, temporary parental anger or disappointment.

This residue of self-doubt or self-loathing undermines our attempt to be confident and effective in our lives. It can obstruct our ability to love and to receive love, and to feel worthy of love. But if we inhabit our chest, we naturally experience the quality of love that dwells there. Then it becomes more difficult to dislike ourselves or to doubt our ability to love and be loved. If we feel the quality of our intelligence in our head, it becomes more difficult to judge ourselves as stupid or to doubt our own insights and understanding. We begin to enjoy the feeling of being who we are, the experience of ourselves as love and intelligence and power and sexuality. This helps us develop a sense of loyalty to ourselves even in difficult encounters with other people.

When we live within the internal space of our body, we begin to know who we are, not from the outside, observing ourselves, but from the inside as a quality-rich experience. We become the subject, looking out at the world around us, rather than the object, seen and judged. All of our lives, we are observed and evaluated. Most children are acutely aware of the way other people are responding to them. In reaction to this awareness of being observed, almost all of us become, to some degree, self-conscious. We worry about whether our words or our body or our behavior will meet with approval. But as we inhabit our body and shift from objectifying ourselves to experiencing ourselves, this self-consciousness dwindles away. We can still tell how others are responding to us, but this awareness is outweighed by our loyalty to ourselves, our experienced knowledge of ourselves. This means that we can gradually let go of our watchful grip on ourselves. We can be spontaneous.

A woman named Charity told me that for all of her life, she had been self-conscious about being "klutzy and ungainly." She said, "I am like a big-footed puppy who never grew up. I've given up all hope of grace. It is just not available to me, despite multitudes of dance classes." It was a revelation for Charity to inhabit her body. She said, "I can experience that there is only me inside my body. When I fill my body with myself, there was no room in it for anyone's critical voices." Charity even found that she began to feel a sense of grace, or harmony within her body, that further quieted her self-criticism. She said, "I can now move my whole body at once so that it actually feels good to move. I feel kind of lovely!"

This basic self-knowledge and loyalty also contributes to our resilience. It helps us recover more easily when another person insults us or when we embarrass ourselves with our own behavior.

When we experience our own existence within our body, we may also feel the preciousness of that existence. This often leads to taking better care of ourselves. We may make better choices regarding food, exercise, rest, environmental stressors, and relationships.

Rachel came to work with me because she had been having thoughts of suicide, but she still had some hope that her life might become livable. Although she was just in her thirties, she had already had several abusive relationships with men. When we met, she had just managed to leave a man who had begun hitting her, and she still had the bruises. This woman grew up in a religious Jewish home. I asked her if she knew any prayers or blessings. "Yes," she said, smiling for the first time since I had met her. "Many. *Berakhah*." The way she smiled when she said the Hebrew word hinted to me that her religion might be a source of healing for her. As I led her through the main embodiment practice, I suggested that she recite a blessing for herself as she inhabited each part of her body. She had broken her ties with her family several years before, after a particularly intense argument, but this practice reminded her of how innocent she had felt as a child in the synagogue. As she made contact with herself in her body, she reported that she could feel her innate innocence and even the "holy fire" within her body. Gradually, she regained the sense of the sacredness of life that she had been taught as a child. After a few months of this practice, along with our verbal dialogue about the pain that she had also suffered as a child, she no longer felt suicidal. And she resolved to find a man to love who would also regard life as sacred.

Grounding in Our Foundation

By inhabiting the body, we regain the natural support of gravity. If we did not feel securely held as children or if we could not rely on the support of our parents, physically or emotionally, it is often reflected as a pulling up away from the base of our body. Emotionally, it may be challenging for us to rely on the support of other people. Physically, we may not be able to rely on the support of the earth, the floor, or the chair to support us. In reaction to trauma, many people uproot themselves; they have the appearance of trying to get up and out of their body through the top of their head or trying to rise above the discomfort of their childhood environment.

Most of us, even if we have not endured severe trauma, live more in the top of our body than the bottom. We may live in our chest, arms, neck, and head but find it difficult to access and inhabit our feet, legs, pelvis, and midsection. This means that we lack foundation, or what is popularly called "grounding." If we have no foundation, we are easily knocked off base, easily overwhelmed by other people or by intense circumstances. We also cannot rest within ourselves. We have a sense of unsettledness, of restlessness, that may limit the degree to which we feel contented and secure in our lives.

When we inhabit our lower body, we feel more connection with the floor beneath us, and we can rely on its support. This helps us let go of the effort that most of us exert in order to keep ourselves upright. The natural support of the ground beneath us can provide us with a sense of security and even help alleviate the psychologically based feeling of insecurity stemming from a lack of support in our childhood. Grounding, in other words, plays an important role in helping us heal from the effects of trauma.

Paula came to work with me specifically to help her with grounding. She told me that when she was a child, her family was constantly moving. Her father had difficulty keeping a job, he was often fired without much notice, and the family would uproot themselves and go to another town where he could start over. Naturally, her father's difficulty in holding on to a job caused a great deal of friction between her parents. Her mother constantly complained that because she could not rely on him to provide for the family, she had no security. Paula felt that this refrain of "no security" had gotten inside her bones. She said that she always felt "wobbly."

Because Paula was so uncomfortable standing, we began our grounding work with her sitting in a chair. I began by asking her to inhabit her feet. When she did that, I noticed that she only inhabited the front of her feet, and only the inner edges of the front of her feet. She pressed down on the floor with the inner edges of her toes and metatarsals but barely touched the ground with her heels or the outer edges of her feet. This imbalance was mirrored, and held in place, by the way she was placed in her hip sockets. She inhabited only the inner edges of her hip sockets, pulling them toward each other in a way that narrowed her pelvis.

When I pointed this out to her, she was able to shift to inhabiting the centers of her hips sockets fairly easily. This shift allowed her to then inhabit both the inner and outer edges of her feet at the same time. Widening in her hip sockets and pelvis also allowed her to settle down, closer to the chair, so she could also inhabit the bottom of her pelvis, the base of her torso. She was surprised at how stable she felt when she inhabited her feet and pelvis in this way.

Since she had mentioned being "uprooted," I also helped her experience dropping roots into the ground. I asked her to find the centers of the soles of her heels. And then to balance her awareness of the centers of the soles of her heels, to find them both at the same time. Then I asked her to find the points right before the metatarsals on each foot and to balance her awareness of these two points. The centers of the soles of the heels are chakras in the Hindu yoga system, and the points before the metatarsals are used in acupuncture, acupressure, and martial arts techniques, where they are called the "kidney 1 points" or "bubbling spring." When Paula had found all four points on the soles of her feet, I asked her to imagine dropping roots down into the ground through those points.

When Paula dropped these roots into the ground, it became clear that there was a strong upward pull away from the ground in her body that seemed to have its source in her forehead. This was a chronic tension in her forehead that maintained the upward displacement and sense of ungroundedness in her body. As we worked to release this tension in her forehead, Paula could feel how, as a young child, she had mirrored her mother's habitual expression of worry. As Paula released this holding pattern, she was able to settle more fully into the foundations of her pelvic floor and her feet.

She then practiced inhabiting her body while standing and walking, with particular emphasis on inhabiting the inner and outer edges of her feet at the same time and inhabiting her hip sockets without narrowing her pelvis. When she was able to maintain this contact with her feet and hip sockets as she stood and walked, I gave her a different practice. I asked her to stand and find the points at the centers of the soles of her heels and the points right before her metatarsals. Then I asked her to imagine dropping roots down through those points, deep into the ground, just as she had done while sitting. When she did this, there was automatically an upward current of energy that rose up through her body and supported her.

Some people feel very heavy when they first practice inhabiting their body while standing. They feel as if they have been glued to the ground. But with practice, we are able to feel that by settling to the ground, there is a spontaneous upward energy that flows through our body and makes it light and buoyant. The more we settle within our body, the more we can experience this upward energy. It is important to understand that this is not a pressing downward. It is the ability to inhabit our lower body, and to rest there.

When Paula sat down again after these standing and walking practices, I remembered her telling me that she had absorbed her mother's refrain of "no security" into her bones. I suggested that she try to feel this lack of security in her bones. Paula was able to inhabit her bones and to feel that even her mother's worried, angry voice seemed to reside there. "It's like a scratchy, harsh feeling inside my bones that keeps me from ever really relaxing," she said. Once she could feel this clearly, she could also breathe this deeply held pattern out of her bones. It took some repeated practice, but eventually Paula was able to feel that there was no longer any worry, anger, or insecurity within her bones. She could inhabit her bones, just as herself. Then she felt that even her skeleton could rest on the ground and support her.

In addition to our particular relationship with our childhood environment, social factors may also cause us to live more in the top of our body than the bottom. Although this is not true of everyone, it is a general pattern in our culture to live "above the belt." "Good" people relate to each other from their heart and heads, but not from "down there." However, when we experience our internal wholeness, we relate to others with our whole being. Our openness to other people, and our responsiveness to them, involves our whole body.

Anxiety also produces an upward displacement in our body. When we are anxious, we rise upward in ourselves, away from our foundation. This upward movement of anxiety is acknowledged in our language with the expression "My heart was in my throat." Many sensitive people grow up with some anxiety and with this anxious, upward displacement in their body. Inhabiting the whole body, including the bottom of the body, can help alleviate a habitual pattern of anxiety.

Our main foundations are our feet and the bottom of our pelvis, or "pelvic floor." When we settle within the foundations of our feet and pelvic floor, we experience grounding, or gravity, throughout our whole being. This helps us feel comfortable and internally cohesive. In the following practice, I also include the foundations of the bottom of our chest, neck, and eye sockets. We can settle within each of these foundations. This is not a downward pressing or a collapsing but an ability to let go and rest within each foundation.

This practice takes only a few moments. If you often feel ungrounded, you can "tune in" on this practice every day until resting within your body feels natural and effortless.

PRACTICE Foundational Grounding

Stand, with your eyes open. If you feel a little shaky standing, you can hold the back of a chair for support. Or you can do this practice sitting.

If you do not need to hold on to a chair for support, let your arms hang loose at your sides. Make sure that you are not trying to support yourself by clenching your fists or tensing your arms.

Inhabit your feet. Feel that there is no separation between your feet and the floor. Experience the foundation of being in your feet. Make sure you are in the whole foundation of your feet, all the way to the backs of the heels. Let yourself rest there within your feet.

Let your breath adjust to you being this far down in your body so that your inhale does not lift you up away from this foundation. Look straight ahead as you do this and allow your vision to adjust to you being this far down in your body so you can live there, in this foundation of yourself.

Each foundation in your body is a foundation for your whole being. Even your mental life has this foundation of your feet. Experience your mental life resting and settled toward your feet. And experience your emotional life resting and settled toward your feet.

Inhabit your pelvic floor. This is the whole bottom of your torso including your sitz bones. Experience the whole rectangle of your pelvic floor. Let yourself experience the foundation of your pelvic floor. Your emotional life rests because you have this foundation, and your mental life rests. And your arms can rest.

Inhabit your respiratory diaphragm, the bottom of your chest. Again, this is a foundation for your whole being. Your emotional life rests because you have this foundation, your voice rests, your mind rests.

Inhabit the bottom of your throat, from your collar bones all the way to the back of your neck. This is an important foundation because we often lift up through the neck. The foundation at the bottom of the neck allows you to settle down through the neck so your voice can rest. Your mental life rests, your arms rest.

Inhabit the bottoms of your eye sockets. Let your eyes rest in the sockets. Do this with your eyes open, as it will change how you look out of your eyes. Let yourself see with your whole eyes, as they rest in the sockets.

Now inhabit all five foundations: feet, pelvic floor, diaphragm, throat, and eye sockets. Walk slowly across the room, inhabiting these foundations. You are walking in this grounded state. Every time you put a foot on the floor as you walk, experience the foundation of being within your foot.

Conclusion

Although anxiety and feelings of insecurity and uprootedness usually originate in reaction to trauma, they can become habitual holding patterns that persist even when our present-day circumstances are calm and secure. Grounding can help us let go of these trauma-based patterns in our body. It can help us experience and express our genuine responses to events in our current lives. For example, resting within the diaphragm as the foundation of our chest connects us to the "bottom of our heart." This is an experience that most of us are familiar with from those moments in our lives when we have expressed something important, with utmost sincerity. When we speak from the bottom of our heart, we actually drop down to the bottom of our chest and the bottom of our throat. This allows us to feel the connection, the internal continuity, between our heart and our throat and to speak our emotional truth.

As we inhabit our body, and learn to rest comfortably within our body, our authentic reception of life and our ability for authentic self-expression becomes an ongoing way of being, an ordinary, everyday reality. Grounding, resilience, self-love, agency, receptivity, and presence are just some of the ways in which inhabiting the internal space of our body helps us heal from trauma and returns us to the birthright of our true nature.

4

THE QUALITIES IN THE BODY

Emptiness is the field in which each and every thing—
as an absolute center, possessed of an absolutely
unique individuality—becomes manifest as it is in itself.

KEIJI NISHITANI

When we inhabit the internal space of our body, we can experience fundamental consciousness pervading our body and environment as a blend of awareness, emotion, and physical sensation. We can also experience a more delineated spectrum of qualities within our body. These qualities seem to be innate—they are uncovered, rather than constructed, as we inhabit each part of our body. They form the experience of a unified ground of our being within which the content of our experience moves.

I do not know what produces the experience of these qualities, so I cannot make any sort of metaphysical assertion about their actual existence. But I do know that we can experience them and that the experience of attuning to each quality is very effective in helping us release the constrictions and patterns of belief and behavior we suffer from trauma.

In the Realization Process, we have specific practices for experiencing each quality within the body. We attune to the qualities of gender (however that feels for each of us) and sexuality within the sexual organs and pelvis, the quality of power within the midsection (between the pelvis and chest), the quality of love within the chest, the quality of voice within our throat, and the quality of intelligence within our head. Since these are qualities, they are experiences and do not fit with the words I have assigned to them in any definitive way. I just use the words that I have found most effective to help people attune to the qualities within their body.

Although we attune to the qualities in specific parts of the body, we can experience all of them pervading everywhere in the body. It is very interesting to experience the quality of love within our legs, for example, or the quality of intelligence within our hands. Just as we can experience fundamental consciousness as a blend of awareness, emotion, and physical sensation, the internal space of our body can be experienced as a blend of all of the qualities of our being. This enriches every aspect of our functioning, bringing timbre to our voice, depth to our touch, intensity to our sexual pleasure, and breadth to our intelligence. The qualities within our body do not need to be cultivated or in any way constructed. They naturally emerge as we make internal contact with ourselves. The integration of these innate qualities of our body form the experiential basis of our wholeness, the internal cohesion of our individual being. Attuning directly to these qualities can help us deepen our internal contact and release the constrictions that we organized within the internal space of our body as children.

The ability to experience these qualities within our body is an important part of reclaiming ourselves from the impact and fragmentation of childhood trauma. For it is these qualities that we tried to control in our organization of ourselves in childhood. For example, if our intelligence seemed to be threatening to a parent or sibling, we may have limited our ability to think by constricting our head. But it is not our head that is the problem; it is our intelligence. Constricting our head is just a means to limiting our intelligence. Likewise, if someone overpowered us, we may have constricted our own power by constricting our midsection. But again, it is not the midsection but the experience of power that we were suppressing.

Most of us grow up barely aware of these qualities in our body. Instead of experiencing the qualities of our aliveness, we may live in an abstract realm of ideas about ourselves, such as "I am a teacher," or "I am a friendly person." Sometimes the recovery of the qualities of our being, the actual feeling of our existence, is fraught with fear of punishment, of breaking taboos. There may also be anger at the necessity for this suppression and grief at the loss of these vital aspects of ourselves. But as we regain ourselves, the richness and distinctness of these qualities are unmistakable. We know that we are intelligent because we can actually feel our intelligence. This means that we may be able to stop telling ourselves that we are stupid, too stupid to accomplish our goals, or too stupid to speak our mind to other people. We know that we cannot be overpowered again because now we can actually feel our own power. We no longer feel less powerful than other people because we can experience the quality of our personal strength within our body. And we know that we are good, that our self-loathing is based on illusion, because we can actually feel the love within our chest.

The Quality of Intelligence

Although people know that they have intelligence, especially if they have it in abundance, not many people experience their intelligence as a quality of being. Once, several years ago, I attempted to present this work to a small group of psychoanalysts in New York City. Every person in the room was strongly suspicious of anything that smelled at all "mystical," and that certainly included an experience of a fundamental, unified ground of consciousness. But one well-respected, very dignified woman took pity on me. These were psychoanalysts, after all, engaged daily in helping people overcome suffering, and seeing me engulfed in this cloud of suspicion, she offered to give my ideas a try.

I knew that this woman had written many books on psychoanalysis, so I decided to begin with her head. I stood behind her and put a hand gently on either side of her head. "Feel that you are between my hands," I said to her. She sputtered a little in protest, but then went ahead and inhabited her head. She gave a little "oh" of surprise as she experienced herself living inside her head. "Now attune to the quality of your intelligence," I said. She laughed and said, "I have no idea what you mean by that." I still had my hands on either side of her head. I said, "See if you can remember the feeling in your head that you have at your computer when you are working on a book and waiting for the next sentence to form." "The feeling of thinking, you mean?" she asked with a trace of sarcasm. Then, catching her tone, she complied with my instruction. The space between my hands became even more alive with this very intelligent woman's intelligence. "Huh," she said, "how strange!"

The quality within the head is not just the feeling of thinking, but the feeling of the potential for thinking. It is the feeling of our intelligence, whether at work or at rest. Inhabiting the body does not mean that you are always aware of this feeling in your head. But attuning to it helps us inhabit our head more fully.

When I teach the attunement to the qualities of our being, I usually use the word "understanding" instead of "intelligence." I have found that if I ask people to attune to the quality of intelligence, they often just inhabit the front of their brain, their forehead. This is where they are most aware of being when they problem solve. So the instruction of the Realization Process practice is, "Inhabit your brain. Attune to the quality of understanding within your whole brain."

People who say that they are "always in their head" or that they need to "get out of their head" usually mean that they experience themselves living in their thoughts. They often feel (and appear) tense in their forehead. Living in our thoughts, or in our forehead, is very different from living in our whole brain. But even our thoughts seem to work better, in the sense of being more original and creative, as we inhabit our whole brain.

When Aline came to work with me, she experienced herself living mostly in her chest. She was a warm, empathic young woman, with an easy affectionate smile. She also had a self-effacing sense of humor that I found both endearing and disturbing. Most of her jokes about herself involved silly mistakes that she had made at work or words that her clever boyfriend had used that she had to look up in order to understand what he was saying. She often shook her head a little at the punchline of these jokes, as if she might dislodge something that had become stuck in her brain.

It was this movement that caught my attention and alerted me to the serious self-suppression that lay beneath her humor. It turned out that she was raised in a family that admired intelligence above all other attributes. Her three older brothers competed for their parents' approval, tossing mathematical proofs and cutting-edge research results around the dinner table in a way that reminded Aline of trained seals. As the baby of the family, and the only girl child, she was not expected to join in the mental acrobatics, and her few attempts were met with gleeful ridicule by her siblings and tolerant amusement by her parents. Now, she often felt what she described as "brain freeze" whenever she had to converse with people she considered to be intelligent. She said that she could feel her brain become rigid.

These movements into contraction often feel like they are being done to us, and we tend to describe them in this way. "My chest became tight," or "My throat closed up." But even though we may not be aware of it, we are doing the moving. With a little practice, Aline was able to feel how she "froze" her brain. It was a subtle, internal movement, but it was still under her control. She was able to find herself as the agent of the movement that contracted her head. She recognized that this was a very familiar movement. She had been contracting her head in exactly this way from early in her childhood, as soon as she became old enough to sit at the dinner table and feel left out of the clever family banter. Having decided, in these early years, that she was stupid, she went on to contract her head whenever a situation arose in which she might have to try and fail to be intelligent. Although the movement seemed to occur spontaneously, and was originally an unconscious movement, she was able to become more aware of when she was doing it. Instead of contracting in this way, she could inhabit her head and actually feel the quality of her own intelligence. After a while, she no longer had to make an effort to do this. She found that she was always living within her whole head, and her mind worked effortlessly. Having been gifted with the same genes as her brothers, she found that people began to appreciate her participation in conversations; they were interested in what she had to say. And she began to enjoy her own intelligence; her own opinions and insights gave her pleasure.

The Quality of Voice

The quality of our voice resides in our throat as our potential to speak. Although not as distinct a quality as the others in the body, it is an important aspect of ourselves to attune to, as it is one of the main aspects of ourselves that we suppress. There are many reasons that children constrict their throat. If we are fed when we are not hungry and crying or saying "no" does not seem to stop that intrusive food-filled spoon, we may tighten all of the anatomy involved in eating in order to defend against it. This includes our lips, mouth, esophagus, and stomach. Later, we may use this same pattern of constriction to fend off other things, such as unwanted affection, or even as part of a pattern to suppress our own sense of longing for affection when we anticipate rejection. We also tighten our throat as part of a pattern to stop ourselves from crying. Very often the throat is constricted as part of holding our breath, in order not to take in the abrasive smells or smoke in the atmosphere, or as part of a fear reaction. It is also very common for us to tighten around our larynx in order to limit our capacity for speech. It is likely that almost all children, at one time or another, are told to be quiet. We can only clamp down on our natural vocal ebullience by tightening the anatomy involved in vocal expression. And some children must tighten their throats against oral sexual abuse.

I remember very well when I first felt the quality of my own voice. It was such an extraordinary event that I can even vividly recall the details of where I was sitting in my New York City apartment and that it was early evening. It was a revelation to me that I could actually feel, in my throat, that I had a voice. As I continued to work with releasing the tensions there, I remembered how shamed I had felt when my immature opinions, as a child and adolescent, had been met with derision by the adults around me. I also came across my mother's reticence to express herself, in her throat and upper chest, mirrored in my own body. For several weeks after I discovered the quality of my voice within my throat, my utterances burst forth from me at inopportune moments, and with inappropriate force and volume. Since I had been a dancer for so much of my childhood and young adulthood, I used to joke that speaking was my second language. So people who knew me were surprised when I began to blurt out loud pronouncements at odd moments. But with time, and continued release, my verbal participation in life took on normal proportions. I channeled my excess verbal impulses into writing. I had often tried to write before but always felt that I was imitating whatever writer I was reading at the time. When I discovered the quality of voice within my throat, I began to feel that I was writing in my own voice and even that my heart and my mind were somehow united within my voice. Then my words began to flow more easily, and this was a great relief for me.

The Quality of Love

The quality of love also appears to be an innate, integral component of our unconstructed being. We discover this quality within our body when we inhabit the internal space of our chest. It is not dependent on an object of love. It can always be experienced as an unchanging, ongoing quality of our being, even when we are alone, without the presence or the memory of a loved person or thing.

Inhabiting the chest and attuning to the quality of love within the chest is a vital aid to recovering from trauma. One of the most common results of childhood trauma is self-loathing. As I mentioned earlier, almost all children blame themselves for the abuse that happens to them. If a parent or other adult, sibling, or peer relates to them with ongoing criticism, they do not yet have the self-knowledge to counter this criticism, and they usually accept the criticism as truth. If they are subjected to fury, violence, or sexual violation, children almost always feel that they deserve this treatment. Perhaps this is because children believe in a just world. Even as adults, it is often challenging for people to regard their childhood selves as innocent victims of the abuse they sustained. They feel that they must have done something to evoke the anger, violence, neglect, abandonment, or lack of love that occurred. But when we actually experience love within our own chest, as a natural quality of our being, that self-loathing often dissipates. It is difficult to maintain dislike or distrust for ourselves when we can feel that we are made of love.

Another common result of trauma is the inability to trust and therefore to love another person. But when we experience the quality of love as part of our own nature, we feel less vulnerable to the possible misbehavior of other people because we can more easily maintain our love for ourselves. We can compare that person's attitude toward us to the feeling of love that we now know intimately within our own body. We also feel less afraid of rejection. We may still feel loss if a relationship ends, but we will not lose love because love is always part of us. This quality of love is a kind of abundance. We can spend freely because it never runs out.

We can use this experience of love within our chest to help heal areas of our body that were the target of abuse. One woman, whom I will call Barbara, had suffered severe sexual abuse as a child and teenager. She described herself to me as "garbage" and "damaged goods." I had never met anyone who looked as battered, or as uncared for, as this woman. Her face was deathly pale, and her hair was lank and greasy. When she sat in my office, she kept her face averted, as if she were hiding from my gaze. Even the way she was dressed seemed an effort to cover up as much of herself as she could.

I led her through the main Realization Process practice of attunement to fundamental consciousness. But we just did the beginning of the practice, in which she inhabited her body. I felt that experiencing the pervasive space of FC might make her feel even more vulnerable and fearful than she already was. I did, however, include attunement to the qualities within the body—the practice at the end of this chapter. When I asked her to inhabit her chest and attune to the quality of love within her chest she pressed both hands to her chest and concentrated her attention there. After a moment, an expression of wonder transformed the usual flat affect in her eyes. "I do feel something," she said. Then she began to cry very softly, like a whimper, and then to laugh at the same time. "I don't know why I'm crying," she said. "But there is something there."

After several months, Barbara was able to experience all the qualities in her body fairly well. She was also able to tell me about the many terrible things that had been done to her. She was able to meet my gaze, to look at me, and to allow me to look at her, while she remained attuned to the qualities of her own aliveness. Then I suggested that she apply the feeling of love within her chest to healing the parts of her body that had been hurt by trauma. She spent the most time sending love to her genitals. Then one day she told me that she felt that her genitals were love. "I can feel the sweetness there," she said.

The Quality of Power

Power is also a felt experience in the body. The quality of power emerges when we inhabit our midsection, between our chest and our pelvis. Power is one of the more challenging qualities for most people to feel. In order to attune to this quality in our body, we need to distinguish it from our associations of the word "power," with the misuse of personal strength that we may see around us in our personal lives and the abuse of social and political strength that we see happening in tragedies around the world.

The quality of power that we can feel in our body is not power over other people. It is not an aggressive feeling. It is pure, natural power, like the power of a waterfall. It gives us a sense of internal buoyancy, vitality, and strength.

Almost everyone suppresses the quality of power to some extent. In general, women are brought up to believe that it is not feminine (not polite) to experience this aspect of themselves. Even though these destructive cultural ideas about gender roles have less impact these days, the long legacy of suppression of power, and constriction within the midsection of the body, is still mirrored, to some extent, by each successive generation of girls. In unconscious imitation of their mothers, girls may organize themselves to be powerless, even though the contemporary circumstances of their lives allow them to feel power.

Men often also suppress power in reaction to gender stereotypes, in which male power is portrayed as abusive and dominating. They fear that if they allow themselves to feel power, they may become those abusive men themselves. Just as women have been taught, for centuries, that power is unattractive in a woman, men have been taught, in our current society, that male power is unattractive and threatening.

Both men and women may have trauma-based reasons for suppressing power as well. We will constrict this aspect of ourselves if we have been bullied or overpowered through verbal or physical abuse. We will also constrict our power as a way of limiting our vitality as children if our parents seem burdened or challenged by it.

When we do not experience the quality of power in our body, we often continue to feel overpowered by other people as adults, even if they are not being abusive toward us. We may feel easily intimidated by other people in our ordinary interactions with them. Some people defend against this vulnerability by attempting to produce a facsimile of power in other parts of their body, for example by pushing forward with their forehead or their upper chest. Although this compensatory organization may be intimidating to others, it is a defensive artifice and does not truly feel like strength. As with any created organization in our body and being, it is also exhausting to maintain, even if we are not aware that we are holding ourselves in this way.

Our actual quality of power requires no effort; it is just naturally there within our body. Although we can intensify it in a particularly challenging situation (we have a kind of "dimmer button" on all of these qualities), it is generally a settled, gentle feeling of personal strength rather than an active state. As an internal quality, rather than an outward attitude, we can rest on or in our own power. This allows us to feel equal to other people, without effort, and to feel supported by our own inner strength.

Since power is a quality, an experience, it is difficult to convey to others verbally and still more difficult to help them attune to it. However, I have found one way that often works. In a recent workshop, Louise asked me to help her attune to the quality of power. She said that she had no idea what I meant by this quality and that she could not begin to experience it. I brought my chair across the room to sit in front of her. Then I asked her to inhabit her midsection. Although she was not used to being in contact with herself in this part of her body, she was able to find this area and to inhabit it. The slight contraction of herself in her midsection released a little as she inhabited it.

"Okay," she said. "But I still don't feel any sort of power there."

"Now," I said, "I am going to attune to the quality of power within my midsection, and you see if you can match me in your own midsection." When I attuned to the quality of power within my own body, Louise hesitated for only a moment and then attuned to the quality of power within her own body. She was surprised and pleased by this new feeling within herself.

"That feels very good," she said.

"Now I'm going to intensify this feeling of power within my body, and see if you can match that. Don't let me overpower you." And I intensified the quality of power within my own midsection. Louise looked apprehensive for a moment but then found that she, too, could intensify the quality of power within her body. We sat for a moment, just enjoying the feeling of being two women, attuned to the quality of power within themselves.

Then Louise looked worried again. "But I don't want to be like this in my daily life," she said. "I want to be loving."

Many people feel that they need to choose between being powerful or being loving. But fortunately, the design of our body means that we can be both at the same time. Within the body, we can experience the quality of love within our chest settling on and being supported by the quality of power within our midsection. The internal continuity between the chest and the midsection means that we experience the quality of love as continuous with the quality of power. There is no separation between qualities and no need to choose between them.

I asked Louise to inhabit her chest and attune to the quality of love within her chest. Then I asked her again to inhabit her midsection and attune to the quality of power. She was now also able to do this quite easily.

"Now inhabit your chest and your midsection at the same time," I said. "And attune to your love and your power at the same time."

Louise did this, and then she smiled. "Somehow that makes my love more powerful," she said.

My interaction with Louise in which I helped her to experience the quality of power in her body was not a transmission. It was not because of my own openness to this quality in myself that she was able to feel it in herself. Rather, she matched my quality of power with her own, through her own volition. However, the phenomenon of transmission is always operating in our interactions with other people, especially if one person is much more open in an area of themselves than the other. If we meet with a friend or teacher who is connected to their authentic voice, for example, we may find that we have easier access to our own voice as a result of that encounter. One woman also told me that when she sits in nature, she feels empowered by the power around her in the trees and earth and sky. However, opening through transmission from another person or some other external source is often temporary, unless we can find these qualities ourselves within our own body.

The Qualities of Gender and Sexuality

Gender is one of the foremost topics in our culture today. The emergence of transgendered people as a social and political force has opened an important inquiry into the nature of gender itself. One of the most positive outcomes of this inquiry, in addition to a widening of our culture's acceptance of diversity, is that it has directed our attention to the ways in which we are still limited by antiquated gender roles and stereotypes.

In the Realization Process, part of the Attuning to the Qualities Within the Body practice (described below) is attuning to the quality of gender within the pelvis. The instruction is: "Feel that you are in your pelvis (I also sometimes include genitals in this instruction). Attune to the quality of gender, however that feels to you."

The purpose of this practice is to help people fully inhabit their pelvis and to attune to whatever quality of gender they happen to feel at the base of their pelvis. If a person who looks female to me inhabits their genitals and experiences the quality there as male, that has the same benefit as if they experience the quality there as female. Even if the experience of the quality changes each time one attunes to it, that does not interfere with the intention of the practice. The intention is to feel whatever quality is there so we can more fully inhabit ourselves in our pelvis and genital area. Also, because these are qualities, the particular word that we each attribute to our experience is not important. It is the experience that the body has an internal quality that is important.

Although the inclusion of "gender" in the Realization Process practice often leads to long, spirited conversations, I have kept this instruction in the work because I have observed that many people suppress their experience of gender. Our associations with both genders are so corrupted by the limitations of conventional stereotypes that many people have little interest in including this aspect of themselves in their wholeness. But I think that this determination not to be gendered may point to the particular need for the healing and inclusion of this quality of ourselves.

The purpose of attuning to the quality of gender in our pelvis and pelvic floor is to be able to inhabit and experience ourselves more fully. One of the purposes of inhabiting ourselves more fully is pleasure. Wherever we are in contact with the internal space of our body, we are open and responsive to our environment. We are capable of stimulation and pleasure. It is pleasurable to experience our whole being and to be able to relax in ourselves without the effort of suppression.

It is also a source of strength to inhabit the very base of our torso. This is the foundation of all of the qualities of our being. Whenever we constrict a part of our being, it limits, to some extent, all of our being. This is because all of our qualities pervade everywhere in our body. So to suppress the quality of our foundation in our pelvis also constricts the base of every part of ourselves.

However, since the purpose of attuning to the qualities within the body is to heal and become whole and to find pleasure and strength in one's being, if attuning to the quality of gender is a source of discomfort, it can be eliminated from one's practice. Instead, you can attune to the quality of sexuality within your pelvis.

That said, a little temporary suffering may be tolerated if it is in the service of eliminating long-held prejudices against one's own gender or healing from the social oppression one has suffered from not experiencing oneself as one's biological gender. The quality of gender within the body has nothing to do with the traits of personality and behavior that have been assigned to us by social conventions. For those of us who do identify ourselves as our biological gender, attuning to that quality within our body can help us free ourselves from whatever negative associations and attitudes we may have toward our own being.

When I asked Marisa to attune to the quality of gender in her pelvis, she refused. Although she was not transgendered or two-spirited, she did not want to identify herself as female. She demanded that I substitute a different word for gender, and so I did. I asked her to attune to the quality of her sexuality, which she found much more comfortable. This attunement did not, however, help her to inhabit her pelvis down to the pelvic floor. For this reason, I asked her to imagine what it would feel like to feel female. She did not have to think very long before she answered, "Women are weak and submissive."

Many women fear that they will be weak, passive, or stuck in a nurturing role if they allow themselves to be female. But none of the qualities of our being are weak. These qualities are experienced as aspects of the unbreakable ground of our being. The female foundation of the body and being is as strong and potent as the male foundation.

Another woman I worked with described her new boyfriend as "very balanced, male and female." I asked her what she meant by that. "He is very sweet," she responded.

Men have been just as limited as women by the stereotypes of their gender. Conventional expectations for men have robbed them of their capacity for sensitivity, intuition, and emotional responsiveness. But when we inhabit our body, we find that both genders have the full range of our human capacities: intelligence, self-expression, emotion, power, and sexuality. The male who has become whole can be just as sweet as a woman, and the woman who has become whole can be as powerful as a man.

There is a slight difference between the quality of male and female gender. But this is a very subtle difference and has nothing to do with gender roles. Although male and female gender qualities differ from each other, and also differ slightly from one person to another, the quality of gender is still different enough from the quality of power, love, voice, or intelligence to be felt as a distinct quality in itself.

In addition to our negative associations with our gender, some people resist experiencing this quality because it does not seem spiritual to them. How can the ground of being be male or female, they ask. Many spiritual traditions, especially in the West, have equated spiritual maturity with a genderless or a hermaphroditic state, largely because they see it as a sexless state, a maturity beyond "earthly" needs. However, when we realize fundamental consciousness pervading our body and environment, our individual being is not eradicated—it is revealed more clearly. This is another way of saying that, as we realize FC, we reach deeper, more subtle contact with our individual form, and with all of its needs and desires.

Carl Jung, one of the first psychoanalysts to include spirituality in his model of maturity, taught that men become whole by connecting with their "female side," or anima, and women become whole by connecting with their "male side," or animus. But Jung lived at a time when male and female roles were severely curtailed by social conventions. For Jung, for a woman to get in touch with her maleness meant for her to have access to power, intelligence, and initiative and for a man to get in touch with his femaleness meant that he could allow himself to be emotional, nurturing, and intuitive. But today we know that we are not innately confined to these gender limitations, but rather they have been imposed upon us by long-standing social and economic conditions. For me, Jung's theory of anima and animus promotes an inaccurate understanding that behavioral and personality traits can be categorized as male or female.

Even though the topic of gender is controversial, I continue to teach it as one of our qualities because it is a part of us that is often wounded and suppressed, and that needs healing and reclaiming. Although some of our wounding and constriction in our pelvis is the result of sexual shaming or abuse, these constrictions in our sexuality also deprive us of our experience of gender.

Alex came to work with me because he had difficulty becoming sexually aroused. Although he was attracted to women, he was unable to have sex with a woman because he was rarely able to have an erection. He also said that when he was relating with other men, he often felt somehow inferior, or weaker than them, even though he knew that they had no idea of his sexual dysfunction. "It feels like something is missing in me," he said.

There are many reasons for sexual difficulties in both men and women. Alex was able to feel the quality of sexuality in his pelvis but not intensely enough to affect his genitals. When he attempted to attune to his quality of gender, he suddenly remembered how, when they were both teenagers, his sister would walk around the house almost naked. Alex had been extremely embarrassed, and still felt ashamed as he remembered many years later, at how sexually aroused he became at the sight of his sister's exposed body. He was able to feel how he had managed to solve this problem in his adolescence by constricting his genital area. As he recognized this constriction and was able to release it and inhabit this area of his body, he began to experience the quality of his gender. This contact with himself intensified his experience of his sexuality. He said that experiencing the quality of his maleness transformed his relationships with both women and men. For the first time in his life, he appreciated being in a male body. He was able to be aroused when he was with a woman he found attractive, and he was able to feel equal with other men.

The following are practices for attuning to the three main qualities of fundamental consciousness: awareness, emotion, and physical sensation that can be experienced pervading your body and environment, and then for attuning to the more delineated spectrum of qualities within your body.

PRACTICE Attuning to the Qualities of Fundamental Consciousness

Sit upright with your feet on the floor. Keep your eyes open.

Feel that you are inside your whole body at once. Find the space outside your body, the space in the room. Experience that the space inside and outside your body is the same, continuous space. It pervades you. Experience that the space pervading your own body also pervades your whole environment. Do not move from within your body to do this: attune to the space that seems to already be there, pervading you and your environment.

Attune to the quality of awareness. This means becoming aware of your awareness. Attune to awareness around, within, and way above your head.

Experience the quality of awareness pervading your whole body so that it feels like you are made of the quality of awareness.

Experience the quality of awareness pervading your whole body and environment at the same time.

Attune to the quality of emotion. Attune to the quality of emotion in the middle of your body: your chest and gut.

Experience the quality of emotion pervading your whole body so that it feels like you are made of the quality of emotion. This is not a specific emotion; it is the subtle ground of emotion.

Experience the quality of emotion pervading your whole body and environment at the same time.

Attune to the quality of physical sensation. Come down into the bottom of your torso, legs, and feet to attune to the quality of physical sensation.

Experience the quality of physical sensation pervading your whole body so that it feels like you are made of the quality of physical sensation. Again, this is not a specific physical sensation; it is the subtle ground of physical sensation.

Experience the quality of physical sensation pervading your whole body and environment at the same time.

Now experience the quality of physical sensation pervading your whole body and environment and the quality of awareness pervading your whole body and environment at the same time.

Add the quality of emotion pervading your whole body and environment. At this point, the qualities blend together; they become indistinguishable from each other.

Sit for a moment in this rich field of awareness, emotion, and physical sensation, pervading your body and environment.

PRACTICE Attuning to Qualities Within the Body

This practice can be combined with the attunement to fundamental consciousness practice in chapter 3. In that version of the attunement to FC, whenever the instruction asks you to inhabit a part of your torso, neck, or head, you can include attuning to the quality associated with that part of yourself.

Sit with your back straight and your feet on the floor. Close your eyes. Begin by feeling that you are inside your feet, that you inhabit them. Let your breath adjust to you being in your feet so that your inhale does not lift you up away from them. Now feel that you inhabit your whole body at once. Sit for a moment, living within your whole body.

Now inhabit your pelvis and genital area. Attune to the quality of your gender, however that feels to you, within your pelvis and genital area. Bring your breath down into your pelvis and feel it move through the quality of gender.

Inhabit your midsection, between your ribs and your pelvis. Attune to the quality of your power, your personal strength, within your midsection. Bring your breath down into your midsection and feel it move through the quality of power.

Inhabit your chest. Let yourself settle within your chest so that you feel that you are sitting in your heart. Attune to the quality of love within your chest. This does not need to be a big feeling; just let yourself feel a little of the tenderness within your chest. Bring your breath down into your chest and feel it move through the quality of love.

Inhabit your neck. Attune to the quality of your voice, your potential to speak, within your neck. Bring your breath down into your neck and let it move through the quality of your voice.

Inhabit your whole brain. Attune to the quality of your understanding within your whole brain. Bring your breath straight back through your head on the inhale, and let it release (go wherever it goes) on the exhale. Feel it move through the quality of understanding.

Now feel that you are in your whole body all at once, including your arms and legs, your whole torso, neck, and head. Find the space outside your body, the space in the room. Feel that the space inside and outside of your body is the same continuous space. You are in your body, but you are permeable; the space inside and outside of your body is the same.

Slowly open your eyes and continue to feel that you are in your body and the space inside and outside of your body is the same, continuous space. Without moving at all from with your body, attune to the space pervading your body and everything in your environment, at the same time.

A variation on this practice is to attune to each quality within the specific part of your body and then to feel that quality pervading your whole body. For example: Feel that you are inside your whole brain. Attune to the quality of understanding within your whole brain. Now experience the quality of understanding in your whole body. You can sit for a few moments, experiencing each quality in your whole body.

Conclusion

If you do this practice consistently, several times a week, after a while, the qualities will just be there whenever you bring your attention to inhabiting your body. These are not just qualities; they are also functions. Knowing and embodying ourselves as these qualities gives us more access to our sensual and sexual pleasure, to our ability to respond with personal power when it is called for in our daily interactions, to our ability to feel the spontaneous welling up of love and other emotions in response to other people, to our authentic voice and to the free flow of our insights and creativity.

5

HEALING TRAUMA FROM THE CORE OF THE BODY

The organismic ground is not truly unknowable in that it
may be directly contacted in wider states of awareness.

SHIN'ICHI HISAMATSU

Very bad news," Selene announced, as she burst into my office.
She landed heavily in her usual chair by the window and covered her face with her hands. "I just cannot face it. Oh no, I
really can't." "What is happening?" I asked. "I have to go home for
Thanksgiving," she sobbed, "and he is going to be there."

I knew who she meant. Her uncle, who had molested her almost
every weekend for several years of her childhood. "What am I going
to do?" she demanded. "How can I possibly sit at the same table with
him, and make small talk, and ugh, eat, with him looking at me?"

Selene and I had talked through this major trauma in her life since
we began working together the year before. She had struggled to regain
possession of herself, to inhabit her body, and to know that it belonged
to her. She had learned to tolerate and then even to enjoy her girlfriend's
touch and to surrender to sexual pleasure without being disrupted by
memories of the abuse. She had begun to blossom in her work and relationships and to glow from within as people do when they become whole.

But the thought of facing this man who had violated her was plunging her back into the shattered state, the "scattered pieces of darkness" as she described the way she experienced herself throughout the years of abuse and for many years after it ended. "I'm losing it. I'm losing it," she cried, panic rising in her voice.

"No," I said, "you can't lose it. You are still there in the center of yourself. Come sit up and find yourself there." Selene sat up and gradually deepened her breathing, keeping her gaze locked with mine for support. As she had practiced many times before, she focused inward until she found the subtle core of her body. This is the vertical channel that runs through the innermost core of our torso, neck, and head. From this core, she could feel her whole self at once, and this calmed her. She was in possession of herself. And from this innermost depth of herself, she had perspective. She was deep inside of her own body, and her uncle was outside of her, no longer smashed against her and suffocating her as he was in her memories. She practiced remaining in this core while imagining him in the next room and found that she could stay stable in her core, in contact with herself as she did this. And then finally, she practiced imagining him in the same room, sitting at the same table, and by augmenting her centered position by breathing within this core of herself, she was able to remain there, in control of her own body, and looking at him across the distance between them.

The next time Selene and I met, two weeks later, she told me proudly that she had been able, for most of the time during her Thanksgiving visit home, to remain in the core of herself. "He is so repulsive," she said. "But I stayed present; I did not space out. I looked directly at him, but I didn't feel bound up with him anymore. He can't get to me. I was in my body, and he was over there, completely separate from me."

The subtle vertical core of the body is mentioned in both Hindu yoga, where it is called *sushumna*, and in Tibetan Buddhism, where it is called the "central channel." Both of these spiritual traditions speak of specific points along the channel (called chakras in the Hindu system) that can be focused on in order to cultivate the inherent qualities of our being. Chakras are experienced as sensitive points along the channel where it is particularly easy to enter into the channel as a whole.

The subtle core of the body is important for spiritual awakening because it is our entranceway into the pervasive space of fundamental consciousness. It is also of key importance for psychological healing and maturity. In the Realization Process, we attune to and breathe within points along this subtle core as part of our approach to healing trauma.

Contact with the subtle core of the body facilitates psychological healing in several ways: it is our entranceway into the experience of our individual wholeness as well as our oneness with our environment; it increases our perspective on the changing content of our experience; it helps us disentangle from fixed beliefs, traumatic memories, and harmful relationships; and it refines our focus so we can more effectively and precisely release the trauma-based holding patterns from our body.

We can experience the subtle core of our body as a pathway for the movement of subtle energy from the center of the bottom of our torso, and below, to the center of the top of our head, and above. I call this channel "subtle" because it is not part of the physical body. It is not composed of physical tissues. It cannot be found in an autopsy. However, it has a particular "feel" to it, and it provides us with particular ways of experiencing ourselves and the world around us, which I will describe in this chapter. And it is conceived of as a channel in both Hindu and Buddhist systems.

PRACTICE   The Core Breath

In this practice, we find three points along the subtle core of the body and initiate the breath from within them. There are three main purposes of this practice: (1) to help us contact and live within the whole core of the body so we can open more fully to the pervasive space of fundamental consciousness, (2) to integrate the breath with our energy, and (3) to open us to our most subtle energy within the core and within the whole body.

We can do this core breath anywhere along the core, even above our head or below the center of the bottom of our torso. But in general, in the Realization Process, we work with the center of the head, the heart center, and the pelvic center.

All of these points are found by the way they feel—they have a slightly electrical, vibrational quality. But we need to direct our focus deeply (but without strain) within each section of our body in order to locate this feeling. The center of the head is found approximately between our ears, in the center of the internal space of our head. The heart center is found in the center of the chest, but deep within the core of the body. The pelvic center is in the center of the pelvis (between the second and third chakras; on the level of the *hara* or *tan tien*), but again as deeply inward as you can focus within the pelvis.

The breath that we take within each of these points is very refined or "thin"; both the inhale and the exhale occur within the point. It may at first feel as though you cannot get enough breath in this way. But with practice, you will find that this tiny breath within the point actually fills the whole body with breath, effortlessly. We are not sending the breath into the whole body, but just by breathing within the point, the body fills with a mix of subtle breath and energy.

Sit upright and close your eyes.

Find the center of your head. Just by being in the center of your head, you have access to the internal space of your whole body at once. In other words, just by being in the center of your head, you can feel the internal space of your feet, your hands, your whole body.

Inhaling through your nose, bring the breath into the center of your head. Exhale through your nose. (The breath needs to be subtle, or "thin," to move through your head to the center.)

Now initiate the breath from within the center of the head so that the center of the head draws in the breath. It is as if you have air in the center of your head that you can breathe. The exhale is a release from within the center of the head.

By breathing within the center of your head, you may feel a resonance, a gentle vibration, throughout the whole subtle vertical core of your body.

Find your heart center (in the center of your chest but deep in the subtle core of the body). The heart center enters you into your wholeness. Just by being there, it gives you access to your whole internal space at once.

Now initiate the breath within your heart center. Your exhale is a release from within the heart center. By breathing within your heart center, you may feel a resonance throughout the whole subtle vertical core of your body.

Find your pelvic center, in the center of your pelvis, deep in the subtle core of the body. The pelvic center enters you into your wholeness; it gives you access to your whole internal space.

Initiate your breath within your pelvic center. By breathing within your pelvic center, you may feel a resonance throughout the whole subtle vertical core of your body.

Now find the center of your head again. Find the center of your head and your heart center at the same time. Find all three centers at the same time.

Initiate your breath from within all three centers at the same time. The exhale is a release from within all three centers. If you cannot initiate the breath from within all three centers, make sure that you do not leave out the center of your head. Keep the center of your head breathing and add in the other two as you can. With practice, you will be able to breathe within all three centers at the same time.

By breathing within all three centers, you may feel a resonance, a gentle vibration, throughout the whole internal space of your body.

Open your eyes. Find the center of your head, your heart center, and your pelvic center at the same time. Each of these points feels as if it is in the very center of all your experience. Let yourself experience your environment from this core of yourself. Usually we experience our surroundings from the surface of our body. By shifting to the vertical core of your body, you may experience a deeper perspective on your environment. Continue to initiate the breath from within all three centers at the same time.

Rest your gaze on the floor in front of you or look straight ahead. Attune to fundamental consciousness pervading your body and environment. See if you can feel that the core points help you enter in to the pervasive space. You can let go from within these points and settle more fully into the pervasive space.

Our Entranceway into Wholeness and Oneness

In order to contact the subtle, vertical core of our body, we need to refine and deepen our inward focus with ourselves. The core is not in the center of the body, but back further, toward our spine. Since the core is experienced as a straight line and a healthy spine is not a straight line, it cannot be located either in the spine or in any of the structures of our physical anatomy. We can only recognize it by the way it feels. When we focus inward, from the front of our body, as deeply as we can, we reach an area that has a slightly electrical quality. Just as fundamental consciousness is a lively, luminous stillness, this channel is experienced as a charged stillness at the innermost core of our being. As we become more adept at finding it, we also feel that just by contacting one point along this core, we can experience the whole core, from the top of our head to the bottom of our torso. Just by touching one part of the core, the whole channel "lights up."

Each point along the core is an entranceway into our internal wholeness. Each point enters us into the experience of the unified ground of fundamental consciousness within our body. Just by being in the subtle core of the chest, for example, we have access to the internal space of our whole body at once. Also, the more we inhabit the core of the body, the more fully and vividly we experience the innate qualities of our wholeness: gender and sexuality, power, love, voice, and intelligence. These qualities seem to emanate from this core.

From the core of our body, we feel that we are living in the very center of all our experience. We know ourselves as the unchanging center within all of the constantly changing movement of life. Even in challenging situations with other people, or in personal crises, we can remain in this centered position. We are still responsive to other people, but we are not entangled with them or with old patterns of relating with them. People will often tell me, "I saw my family last week, and when I stayed in my core, my experience was very different. It was as if I could just let them be who they are without getting caught up in the usual drama. And then I could be myself with them." Or, "My husband and I started to get into our usual argument that we always have, but this time, instead of reacting the way I usually do, I stayed in my core. Then I could really see that he was more sad than angry with me, and I responded to that instead of to the anger. And then we actually resolved our argument and felt closer to each other than we have in a long time."

To live within the core of ourselves feels like we are living within the source of our ability to think, to feel, and to sense. All of our responses arise fresh, in the moment, rather than out of our habitual patterns of response.

From this central vantage point, we can receive life without feeling displaced by it. One woman told me that she noticed the biggest effect of inhabiting the core of herself when she walked down the street of her town. Michele described herself as an introvert. She always felt shy when she was out in her small friendly town, keeping her face a bit turned away from the people she passed in the street to avoid having to interact with them. But when she was able to live within the subtle core of her body, that changed. She discovered that from her core, it was no problem at all, it was even pleasurable, to pass people in the street and exchange a friendly greeting with them. "From my core, it all just feels like warmth," she said.

Just as the core of the body enters us into the fundamental, unified consciousness that pervades our individual being, it is our entranceway into FC pervading our environment. To inhabit the core of the body, therefore, is to know ourselves as the pervasive, unified ground of our individual form and our environment at the same time. Inhabiting the core of the body is a crucial requirement for realizing fundamental consciousness. If we do not access this channel, we may have an experience of space or expansion, but it will feel like something separate from ourselves, like an object of our experience. Or we may open to it just through our head and experience it only as awareness. When we inhabit the subtle vertical core of our body, we experience fundamental consciousness (it experiences itself) as our own nature. As I described in previous chapters, FC is not just empty space and not just awareness, but a vibrant, luminous expanse, rich with the fundamental qualities of our whole being.

In the same way that fundamental consciousness is disentangled from the content of our experience, allowing it to flow without obstruction, the subtle core of the body is also disentangled from the movement of experience. This means that as we contact and live within this channel, we can more easily let go of our grip on ourselves and our environment. We can more easily notice and free ourselves from our habitual patterns of experience. And we can more easily let go of the rigid organizations that are bound in the connective tissue of our body. As we let go of ourselves from the core, we find ourselves, more and more fully, in the fundamental ground of our being.

Increasing Perspective

The subtle core of the body is our entranceway into oneness with our environment, and at the same time, it is also our greatest distance from our environment. Inhabiting the innermost core of ourselves increases our perspective, on both our internal experience and our perception of the world around us. This perspective gives us a sense of scale so we are less overwhelmed by ordinary irritations. It allows us to see the "big picture" of whatever circumstance we find ourselves in. It can also help us put our memories of our traumatic past into perspective so we can gradually accept and accommodate that these things have happened to us, that they are part, but not all, of our history. From the vantage of the core of our body, neither our present nor past impinges on us with the same force; we have space to breathe and to more clearly perceive whatever is happening or whatever has happened.

This deepened perspective helps us notice when we slip into old reactive or defensive patterns of behavior, which we developed in response to trauma, large and small. This, in turn, gives us the choice to react differently to situations that have triggered these patterns in our past.

In reaction to trauma, we may hold chronic feelings of anxiety, fear, sadness, or anger in our body that influence our mood. Although we may not be able to trace these chronic emotional states to their specific traumatic origins, they still color our experience of ourselves and our world. If we hold grief in our body, for example, we may experience that life is basically sad, and we see the sadness in everyone we meet. If we hold anger or fear in our body, life may seem inherently frightening or frustrating, a constant battle. These moods also influence our habitual thought patterns, which in turn serve to maintain our mood, resulting in an endless cycle.

A more spacious perspective can enable us to recognize our habitual mood-producing thoughts and help free us from our chronic emotional states. Severe mood disorders, such as severe depression, mania, and bipolar disorder, are usually caused by chemical imbalances or other brain dysfunctions and need to be treated with medication. But more ordinary levels of depression and anxiety are often sustained by repetitive thought patterns. If you say to yourself, "I am happy," you may notice a temporary lightening of your mood. If you tell yourself, "I will never get my work done on time," you may notice a slight anxiety in your body, even if that phrase has no relevance to your current circumstances. If you tell yourself, "I am ugly," you may notice a lowering of your mood. People with chronic depression and anxiety often keep up a steady and largely unconscious inner monologue of negative ideas. They may immerse themselves in self-hating thoughts that denigrate their appearance, their intelligence, or their chances at finding or keeping love or achieving success in their work.

I knew one very intelligent woman who kept herself in a state of debilitating anxiety by telling herself constantly that she was stupid. She was so used to this taunting internal voice that she barely registered its presence. But when she attempted to sit still and not think for a few minutes, she was amazed that it spoke up every few minutes. "No wonder I'm having trouble completing my dissertation," she said.

Chronic negative moods can be healed by changing our thoughts. But anyone who has ever tried to "think good thoughts" for any length of time knows how extremely challenging that is. At best, it is a kind of brainwash that holds us in a static mental state, making it difficult for us to have any spontaneous thoughts at all, either good or bad. It cloaks our obsessive or negative thoughts without actually eradicating them. They may still break out of hiding in unguarded moments.

A more effective cure for troublesome thoughts is perspective. If we can gain perspective on our thoughts, we can observe them without becoming involved in them (without believing them). We can sometimes even detect the triggers for these thoughts. Then we can address the triggers themselves rather than trying to suppress our thoughts. Once our tape loops of habitual thoughts start, they move along well-worn grooves and are difficult to stop. But if we can notice, in the moment that it happens, the event that initiated this onslaught, such as the glance at our reflection in a shop window, a disapproving expression, or comment from a relative or colleague, we have a chance to reason with ourselves and resolve our reaction to the triggering event.

By gaining perspective on our habitual thought patterns, we may even be able to discover the origin of these negative thoughts in our childhood history—how we began to doubt our abilities or to denigrate our own intelligence or appearance. We have a chance to link our depression to old feelings of being unloved or rejected, or our anxiety to the threats of disapproval or violence in our childhood home or peer environment, and then possibly to recognize that these circumstances no longer exist in our lives. We may be able to feel how we constricted and held these emotions in our body in reaction to childhood events and release them from our body so we are no longer haunted by the emotions of our past.

We can gain this perspective on our thoughts through a practice of observing them. Many meditation practices are designed to do exactly this. Some meditations, especially those meant for beginners, attempt to stop the flow of habitual thought patterns by stopping thoughts altogether. There is a beginner's Zen meditation in which the meditator is meant to count their exhales from one to ten, going back to "one" each time they have a thought. In practice this is more like repeating the mantra of "one" over and over. However, it does alert you to the amount and types of thoughts you have, usually without even noticing them. For example, we may engage in a verbal feud with a friend or family member all day long without paying attention to it or even noting our tension and anger.

The act of observation itself can help interrupt and dissolve our repetitive tape loops. But eventually, it is not necessary to attempt to stop our thoughts. More advanced meditations instruct us to observe the passage of our thoughts without becoming caught up in them.

They use metaphors such as allowing the thoughts to pass through our mind like fish through the sea or birds through the sky. Observing our thoughts, rather than becoming caught up in them, makes a more spacious medium of our mind. This is an actual spatial shift, an expansion of awareness, and a deepening of perspective. But this "non-grasping" onto our thoughts can take many years to cultivate. In the Realization Process, the practice of contacting and inhabiting the subtle core of the body can facilitate and accelerate this ability.

Refining and Integrating Our Breath and Energy

In the Realization Process, I make a distinction between the experience of ourselves as matter, energy, and fundamental consciousness. These are three levels of subtlety or refinement in our attunement to ourselves and our environment, with matter being the least subtle and fundamental consciousness being the most subtle. As matter, we feel completely separate from the world around us. We have little inward contact with ourselves, except for some awareness of our breathing or when emotion or physical pain draws our attention to our body.

Many sensitive people experience themselves as energy, the streaming, vibrating, pulsating aspect of our being. As energy, we often feel not only one with the world around us but merged with it. Although this merging can be pleasant, it also means that we easily lose our inward sense of ourselves, of our own needs and preferences, in relationships with others. We may also be easily overwhelmed by the world around us, as if we were blown about by the winds of sensory and emotional stimuli.

When we realize ourselves as fundamental consciousness, we know ourselves as the stillness pervading the forms of matter and pervading the movement of energy. We can then experience that energy moves through us without altering our basic identity.

The energy system itself is designed on a spectrum from dense to subtle. As fundamental consciousness, we experience the most subtle range of our energy system. This subtle vibration is experienced everywhere in the body at once. The subtle core of the body is therefore not only our entranceway into the internal wholeness and self-other oneness of fundamental consciousness. It also opens us to the most subtle energy of our being.

When we are able to breathe within the subtle core of our body, as in the previous Realization Process practice, we integrate our physical breath with our energy system. Instead of just breathing with our lungs, we feel that we are breathing within our whole body at once. For example, we experience the internal space of our feet breathing at the same time as we experience the internal space of our head breathing. There is energy and breath everywhere in our body. We can experience the stillness of fundamental consciousness and the subtle vibration of the breath and energy at the same time, everywhere in our body. This helps us feel buoyant throughout our whole being.

Everywhere that we inhabit the internal space of our body, our energy moves freely. The more we know ourselves as the stillness of fundamental consciousness, the more freely, deeply, and fluidly our energy moves. When we constrict our body, we bind not only the physical tissues of our body, but also the energetic aspect of our being. Wherever we have constricted ourselves, we cannot experience the flow and vibration of our energy system. But as we release these constrictions, we gain not only more of the internal ground of our being, but also a fuller energetic experience of ourselves. This internal fluidity, as it becomes free to flow throughout our whole body, is the basis of our felt sense of vitality and aliveness.

PRACTICE Core Breath with Subtle Circuitry

The purpose of this practice is to help you open to the subtle energy and therefore more fully to the pervasive space of fundamental consciousness throughout your whole body.

Sit upright with your feet on the floor. Close your eyes.

Find the centers of the soles of your heels. Balance your awareness of these two points.

Find the centers of the soles of your heels in a way that produces an automatic resonance in your hip sockets. You may also feel a resonance in the centers of your knees as you do this.

Find your shoulder sockets. Balance your awareness of the space inside your shoulder sockets.

Find your shoulder sockets in a way that automatically produces a resonance in the centers of your palms. You may also feel a resonance in the centers of your elbows as you do this.

Find the center of your head. Initiate the breath from within the center of your head, feeling a resonance through your whole vertical core and in the whole circuitry of points in your arms and legs.

Find your heart center. Initiate the breath from within your heart center, feeling a resonance through your whole core and in the whole circuitry of points in your arms and legs.

Find your pelvic center. Initiate the breath from within your pelvic center, feeling the resonance through your whole core and in the whole circuitry of points in your arms and legs.

Find the center of your head again. Find the center of your head and your heart center at the same time. Find the center of your head, your heart center, and your pelvic center at the same time. Initiate the breath from within all three centers, feeling the resonance throughout the whole circuitry of points in your arms and legs.

Now inhabit your whole body. Let yourself experience that the whole internal space of your body is breathing. The same subtle breath and energy that you may have felt in the core points is now everywhere in your body.

Open your eyes. Continue to inhabit your whole body, and to feel the subtle breath and energy everywhere in your body.

PRACTICE   Opening to the Upward Current of Energy

This is a practice for attuning to the upward current of energy through the subtle vertical core of the body. To experience this upward current may require some repeated practice over time. If you are patient and consistent in your practice, you will eventually experience it.

The upward current is experienced as a fine, thin "thread" of energy. Sometimes people experience the energy in the core as a powerful upward whoosh, but that is just an initial opening experience. With a more subtle focus, you can find the very subtle threadlike energy. This is a calm ongoing fluidity within the core of the body. Although there is also a downward energy through the core, in the Realization Process, we just open to the upward current. The downward current will occur as a result of opening to the upward current without requiring any specific attention to it.

Sit upright with your feet on the floor. Close your eyes.

Feel that you inhabit your feet. Let your breath adjust to you being within your feet so your inhale does not lift you up away from them. Feel that are in your whole body.

Now inhabit your pelvis. Fill your whole pelvis with yourself.

Find the center of the bottom of your torso. Open this area and receive an upward current of energy into your pelvis. Do not pull this energy up or imagine it. Just open to it and wait for it to come up. Receive the current within your pelvis.

Now inhabit your midsection, between your pelvis and your chest. Find a point in the core of your midsection by focusing inward in this area as deeply as you can, without strain.

Open this area in the core of your midsection and receive the upward current. It can also help to experience the point in the core settling gently downward in order to help the upward current rise.

Inhabit your chest. Find a point in the innermost core of your chest. Open and settle this point and receive the upward current in your chest.

Inhabit your neck. Find a point in the innermost core of your neck. Open and settle this point and receive the upward current in your neck.

Inhabit the center of your head. Open and settle this point and receive the upward current in your head.

Now you can let the current keep moving upward and out through the center of the top of your head. Keep the top of your head gently settled to allow the current to move through it.

Find the center of the bottom of your torso again, and let yourself experience the current moving upward through the whole subtle core of your body and out through the top of your head. The more you can be relaxed and settled within your body, the more easily the current will rise through the core of your body.

You can also find the centers of the soles of your heels and open those points to the subtle upward current. Receive the energy, and allow it to move up through your legs and to join with the upward current at the center of the bottom of your pelvis, where it continues to rise up through the subtle vertical core of your body.

You can do this practice sitting or standing, opening to the upward current at the centers of the soles of your heels and the center of the bottom of your pelvis.

Most people, when they first inhabit their body, describe a feeling of lightness and spaciousness. But others are surprised to feel heavier than they did before. If we have been living mostly in our upper body and even above our body, as many of us do, then inhabiting our whole body may feel, initially, that we fixed too firmly to the ground. As one person put it, "Now I am so grounded that I may never move again." The upward current of energy can help the body feel buoyant and supported. When we open to it, sitting and standing upright require much less effort.

Conclusion

To live within the subtle vertical core of the body feels like the deepest contact that we can have with our individual being. It enables us to feel that we are alone with our experience, relatively free from the influences of others so we can know what we really think, feel, and perceive. It allows us to survey and experience our environment and other people *across distance* so we do not feel overwhelmed, intimidated, or entangled with them. At the same time, it is our entranceway into a felt experience of oneness with other people. It also allows us the refinement of focus and breath with which to enter into the most constricted parts of our body and being, and bring them back to life.

6

FREEING THE SENSES
FROM TRAUMA

No longer do finite objects appear as separate
and limited structures; rather, the silent and
translucent consciousness out of which all things
are composed surfaces and becomes visible
as the true reality of perceived objects.

PAUL MULLER-ORTEGA

Much of our childhood trauma involved and impacted
our senses, causing us to constrict them. Our environment may have been abrasive, painful, or confusing in
the ways it looked and sounded, in the smells and tastes to which
we were subjected, in the ways we were touched and handled, and
even in the textures of our clothes against our sensitive skin. Just as
in other areas of our body, the constrictions that we created as children in the organs of our senses hold the memory and emotions of
the specific stimuli that we protected ourselves against. Many of our
traumatic memories are complex. We may, for example, be screamed
at by our father and at the same time, smell his sweat so that the
sound, the noxious odor, and our own terror at being the object of
his fury all become bound within our body. As adults, we may feel

alarm and terror when we smell sweat, or we may feel nauseated when we are yelled at, in the same way that we were sickened by our father's smell when he yelled at us.

We do not only constrict our senses in reaction to trauma. We also mirror the constrictions in our parents' senses. And we constrict our senses in order to concentrate. Especially as children, when we must learn a great deal very quickly and then be tested on it, it may be necessary that we narrow our vision and our hearing in order to accurately take in and memorize what is being taught to us. Or we may need to blot out the sounds or even the smells in our environment that interfere with our ability to study or do our homework. We may also constrict our senses so as to better concentrate on an unpredictably traumatic childhood environment. For example, it may be crucially important for our survival that we hear the exact tone in our parent's voice when he or she calls out to us or that we hear our older sibling's approach to our room as we lie in our bed at night. In these ways, we develop habitual and then chronically held limitations in our perception. As we release the constrictions from our senses, the world around us becomes more vivid, more tangible, and at the same time, more transparent.

There is a Zen story about a monk and his teacher who were walking in their monastery garden. The monk says, "An ancient master said that the whole universe is of one and the same root as my own self. What does this mean?" The teacher pointed to a rose that had just come to full bloom. He said, "Most people see this flower as in a dream."

In the beginning of this book, I described fundamental consciousness as the basis of our most direct, unfiltered contact with ourselves and our surroundings. An important aspect of our contact with our environment is sensory perception. As a pervasive expanse of consciousness, FC is also a perceptual expanse. As we realize ourselves as FC, our environment is revealed with greater clarity. As the "near side" of our subjectivity, there is less projection, less "dream." Just as we experience ourselves as more real, more authentic, the world around us also appears to be more as it really is. We have the sense, as it has been described in Zen Buddhism, that we are looking "directly at it."

Since it is the role of the senses to be open to the environment, we very often constrict the senses in childhood in order to lessen the impact of our environment. Even sensory stimuli that are not emotionally laden can be abrasive and overwhelming to a child. The buzz of a kitchen appliance, the vivid colors in a painting that is hung on a bedroom wall, or the smell of smoke can be irritating or feel threatening to a child.

One of Carol's main traumatic memories was of riding in a car full of cigarette smoke when she was around seven years old. As an adult, if she smelled even the slightest whiff of smoke, she would feel panic, as if she were suffocating. Whenever she spoke of that smoke-filled ride in the car, which she did often, she intensified the chronic holding pattern in her nose, throat, and lungs. Since she kept returning to this one specific memory, we explored what else might have occurred around that same time or in that car but found nothing out of the ordinary. However, as she worked with allowing the constriction in her breathing to intensify and then release, she realized that this scene was emblematic of a childhood filled with the secondhand smoke from her parents' excessive use of cigarettes. It was on that car ride when she was seven that she began to equate the foul-smelling smoke that so often surrounded her with her father and mother smoking in the front seat. She had to return many times to working with her deeply entrenched pattern of constriction in her respiratory anatomy before she could trust the air around her and allow herself to breathe freely.

The senses are also susceptible to hijacking. Greta told me that when she was a child, she was intrigued by a statue in her father's office of three monkeys in different postures, one covering his eyes, one his ears, and one his mouth. "What are they doing?" she asked. "The monkeys represent see no evil, hear no evil, speak no evil," her father said. She retained a vivid memory of this conversation, but it was not until several decades later that she understood the relevance of these injunctions in her own life. The restraint practiced by these poor monkeys figure prominently in many of the childhoods described to me in the course of my work. "We are a happy family, a perfect family" the monkeys say. "Anything else you may perceive here or wish to express here is entirely without validity." Children can easily be made to doubt or deny their own perceptions when they do not match what they are told. In reaction to this dissonance, they may suppress their perception and their understanding, and the link between their perception and understanding.

The emotions and memories held in our senses color the world that we perceive as adults. I worked with a man who had been trying to overcome his chronic depression for many years. Leslie told me right away that his present life was very satisfying. He loved his wife and his children, and he felt fulfilled and successful in his career. He also said that he did not want to talk about his childhood, that he had been over every inch of his memories with several therapists and still felt no relief from his depression. "But you have to admit that it's a very sad world we live in," he said. "Everywhere I look, people are unhappy."

When I led Leslie through the attunement to fundamental consciousness practice, he was able to inhabit his body easily. He even felt some happiness as he inhabited his chest, but it was quickly replaced with his chronic sorrow. It was not until we reached his face in the exercise that I was able to see the rigid binding of this sorrow in his eyes. Although his eyes were deep and expressive, with many changing expressions, they also contained a static band that seemed like the sadness of a young boy. I asked Leslie if he was able to locate the feel of this bound sadness in his vision. With careful, attunement, he was able to isolate this feeling in his eyes, and then his whole body became suffused with grief.

"What are you seeing?" I asked. "My father is beating my mother," he said, sobbing. "She is cowering on the floor beneath him, and he is attacking her with his fists."

"I always knew that he beat her, I've talked about it in therapy so many times. But I've never actually seen it like this before. It's as if I'm right there, watching. And it's so sad. I feel so helpless and sad."

Leslie and I worked for a while with him attuning to this part of his vision, where he had held on to this terrible memory, and feeling the sadness that he felt as a young boy, and then, using the method that I will describe in chapter 8, releasing the vision of his parents. This allowed his eyes to become clear and the sadness to dissipate. He began to feel lighter, and his eyes appeared deeper and clearer. "Everything looks brighter," he said.

Nora came to a workshop complaining of pain in her shoulder. "I feel like I'm carrying all of the world's problems on my shoulders," she said, and she rolled her shoulders uncomfortably. "I can't even bear to watch everyone in the group do their work; I just can't stand to hear another person cry." We started our work together with the tension in her shoulder, the one that was giving her the most pain. She let it constrict and release. On the constriction, her left ear seemed to be pulled toward her shoulder. "I've been getting ringing in that ear," she said. So we switched to working with her ear, letting it constrict and release. When she focused within the tension in her ear, her hearing seemed to extend way out into the space to the left of her. It seemed that the tension in her ear was holding a pattern of hypervigilance in her hearing. As she let that happen, she suddenly gasped and began to cry. "What do you hear?" I asked. "I hear the baby crying downstairs," she said.

She had grown up in a large family, and her parents were often unable to cope with the demands of the family. As the oldest child, she felt responsible for both her harried parents and for her five younger siblings. "I remember lying in my bed at night, trying to sleep, but always listening for anyone who might need me. I always had one ear open to the rest of the house." Once she had recognized this source of the tension in her ear and shoulder, it was easier for her to allow it to go into the constriction and to experience the intense pattern of listening for sounds of distress and then to release it. After several repetitions of this, she said that it was quiet within her head for the first time in years. The persistent ringing had stopped.

I have mentioned how being fed when not hungry can, if repeated, lead to chronic constriction in the parts of our anatomy that are involved in eating. But our sense of taste can also be traumatized and result in similar constrictions. Once I was sitting in a restaurant, observing the couple at the table next to me. They both seemed raucously drunk, while their young infant slept peacefully in a carrier by their feet. But at one point, in high spirits, the father dipped his finger into his whisky and then slipped his finger into the sleeping infant's mouth. The baby woke and swallowed convulsively, then contracted his esophagus as it was assaulted by the burning, strong-tasting liquid.

At the same time, he lifted his gaze to his parents laughing faces. I had the impression that he was trying to make sense of these two conflicting sensory experiences: his parents' laughter and the painful sensation in his mouth and throat.

Many children close off their sense of touch when they are handled roughly, physically abused, or forced to touch or be touched by another person sexually. This constricting of our tactile sense may limit both our capacity to experience being touched and to feel what we are touching. A woman came to work with me a few years ago who had constricted her sense of touch as a protection against the lack of stimulation, or contact, within the touch that she experienced as a child. Lisa shone from within her body like a bright light yet seemed almost incorporeal. I found it interesting that she could be so present and yet so disembodied. As I sat with her and listened to her speak, I realized that she had constricted her skin while leaving much of her internal presence intact. Her skin was so contracted that it was almost like she didn't have any. Although she was young, there was something withered about her. I was not surprised when she told me that she had never been in a close relationship and wasn't sure that she wanted one.

As she spoke about her childhood, a picture emerged of an extremely sensitive and contactful child being raised by parents who were barely capable of any contact. Although Lisa sensed that they loved her, she experienced them as so remote and subdued that her interaction with them left her feeling isolated and untouched. Even when they actually touched her, they still felt remote, as if they could not quite reach her. As she said this, Lisa pulled in her skin even more, so that I could see, and finally Lisa could feel, the specific movement of this constriction. It looked as if she was closing her pores. I had the thought that, without the outer coating of skin that most people had, she seemed both untouchable and painfully exposed and vulnerable. I suggested that she imagine having fur. "What kind of fur?" she asked. "Any kind you'd like," I said.

As I watched, Lisa grew imaginary but luxurious fur. She slowly transformed herself from a shriveled pseudo—old lady to a sensual young woman. "Wow, that feels great!" she said. The imagined fur enabled her to relax into the surface of herself, to fill up the envelope of her skin so that she now seemed larger. Having this extended, furry surface helped her feel safe to open to the experience of touch. "I can feel the breeze from the window on my arms," she said. "It feels amazing." I do not know if she was even aware that she had begun to stroke the upholstery of the chair with her fingertips, but I did not want to interrupt her exploration of this new realm by asking her.

Increasing Our Sensory Experience

The senses reflect and reveal the way we inhabit our body as a whole. When we live more in the top of our body than the bottom, we look out of the top of our eyes. This does not mean that we look upward, but rather that we are positioned to see out of the top third of our eyes. This affects what we see. It affects the appearance of our world. When we live in the mid-third of our body, we look mostly out of the mid-third of our eyes. When we live mostly in the bottom of our body, in physical sensation, we look mostly out of the bottom third of our eyes.

You can test this out for yourself by taking a moment to inhabit your whole body. Bring your focus to the curtains in your room or the carpet. Let yourself see the texture of the curtains or carpet. As you do this, notice what happens within your body. You may notice that you naturally drop down to the bottom of your body in order to perceive texture.

When we live in our whole body at once, we see more aspects of the world around us, we receive more of the picture. The more contact we have with the internal space of our body, the more fully we can see, hear, touch, taste, and smell the world around us. We also become open to a subtle range of sensory experience. We may be able to see light emanating from living forms for example, or to hear the very subtle buzz of the energy in the air.

Expanding Our Perception

The constrictions in our senses are tensions. They limit our perception, and they also strain it. Our constricted senses work harder to perceive than our relaxed senses. They grasp on to the objects of our perception.

All of the constrictions in our body form a protective barrier between ourselves and the world around us. They divide the space between self and other. This includes the constrictions in our senses, which serve to protect and divide us from the objects of our perception. In spiritual teachings, this divided self-other space is called "duality," and the expanded space of self-other unity is called "nonduality."

The divided self-other space is a shrunken space. As those constricted parts of ourselves, we are bound up with the objects that we are protecting against. We are both divided from the world and bound up with it. When we realize ourselves as fundamental consciousness, we let go of this bound-up, divided relationship with our environment. We become disentangled from our surroundings as we experience oneness with our surroundings.

Our constricted senses shrink our world. They separate us from the objects around us, but they also bring those objects closer to us than they really are. As we heal from trauma, we live in a more spacious world. This means that as we let go of the constrictions in our senses, we experience deeper perspective, called "depth perception." Objects seem further away, but at the same time clearer, as if we are finally seeing them as they are.

In Buddhism, this clarity has been called "suchness." If we regard the cup on our desk, for example, with relatively unfettered senses, we are able to perceive the suchness, the "cupness" of the cup. We wake from the dream of the cup, shadowed by chronically constricted ways of seeing, and the projection of a thousand other cups that we have "sort of" seen before, and we regard the cup as that very specific cup.

We may have a cognitive and emotional experience of the cup in this awake state. When we know ourselves and our surroundings as fundamental consciousness, our thoughts and emotional responses to what we perceive do not interfere with our direct perception. We may think *cup, my favorite cup*, or *that cup is a little dirty*. We may have an emotional response to the cup, a feeling of love for our favorite cup or anxiety as we realize how many cups of coffee we have had that morning. But these cognitions and emotions occur in present time. They appear cleanly and fluidly in the space of FC along with our perceptions.

This may be self-evident for most readers, but some spiritual teachings claim that an awakened state is just the sensory experience without any thought or emotion. This idea of spiritual realization strips the world of its richness, but more importantly, it actually limits our realization of ourselves as the unified ground of fundamental consciousness. It fragments our internal wholeness, divorcing our perception from our other human capacities, thus increasing the schism between self and object. So it is important to understand that the suchness of the cup does not require that we suppress our mental and emotional responses to our environment.

When we know ourselves as fundamental consciousness, perception becomes less effortful. We can let go of our grasp on the objects of perception and allow them to simply appear in our perceptual field. We experience that fundamental consciousness is doing the perceiving. Of course, we are each still the agent of our own perception, since fundamental consciousness is experienced as our own nature, not something separate or different from ourselves. But instead of going out toward the objects or drawing them closer to us, the objects of our perception seem to arise directly out of the clear space of fundamental consciousness. We do not have to listen in order to hear or to look in order to see.

As fundamental consciousness, our senses also seem to function in a more unified manner. Experientially, this means that we have a single, multisensory perception of our surroundings that appears to emerge without our volitional effort.

The shift that occurs in our perception as fundamental consciousness that many people find the most surprising is the capacity to see within other forms in nature. As the perceptual expanse of fundamental consciousness, all objects appear to be permeable, to be made of space. With an inanimate object, such as a chest of drawers, even though it appears to be permeable, we cannot see what is in the drawers. And even though the walls of the room seem to be pervaded by space, we cannot actually see whatever is on the other side of the walls. But with living objects, such as trees, animals, and people, we can, to some extent, actually see and feel the life within them. This seems to be a combination of seeing and touching, a combination of our visual and tactile senses. I call it "see-feel," but I am using the word "feel" to mean tactile experience, rather than emotion.

If we experience fundamental consciousness pervading both our own body and a tree at the same time, for example, we can see-feel the vibrancy, the force of life, within the tree. If we perceive an animal in the same way, we may be able to detect something of what it is like to be that animal—we may be able to see-feel the quality of that animal's intelligence, emotional experience, and physicality.

When we perceive a human being in this way, we receive even more nuanced information. We can, to some extent, perceive where a person is most open in their body and where they are constricted. We can see-feel what emotions they are currently feeling and even what emotions are chronically bound in their body, along with the feel of the age or ages at which they became bound. We can see-feel, to some extent, what it is like to be that person—the particular quality of that person's intelligence, love, and physical sensation.

Occasionally people in my workshops protest that it is not polite or appropriate to look at another person this deeply. I do not agree with this. We do not need another person's permission to really look at them. Whenever we look at another person, we see more than they are intending or aware of showing us. I believe that it is appropriate for us to cultivate our sensitivity to the world around us and to see people as deeply as we can. This is part of our knowledge of the world and part of our intimacy with other people. And it is also part of realizing ourselves as fundamental consciousness. But it is important that we use what we see with compassion and restraint, and always keep in mind that our perception might be wrong.

The Tibetan Buddhist teacher Chögyam Trungpa Rinpoche once said that "compassion is seeing through confusion." When we see-feel within another human being, we can sometimes see through their layers of protective and compensatory constrictions and perceive the person that they truly are within this binding. Often this evokes in us a recognition of our basic kinship with other human beings and a spontaneous upwelling of compassion for the ways in which we have all hidden and confined ourselves.

PRACTICE Perception as Fundamental Consciousness

Sit upright with your feet on the floor and your eyes open.

Feel that you are inside your whole body at once. Find the space outside of your body, the space in the room. Now experience that the space inside and outside your body is the same, continuous space. It pervades you. Bring your breath smoothly and evenly through the space. Experience that the space that pervades your body also pervades the objects in your room and the walls of your room. Stay in your whole body as you experience this.

Experience that all of the sounds you hear are just occurring in the space without changing the space.

Experience that the space itself is hearing the sounds. You do not have to listen in order to hear. The hearing happens by itself. You are receiving the sounds, without any effort.

Now allow everything that you see to just be in the space without changing or altering the space.

Experience that the space that pervades your whole body also pervades your eyes. Your eyes are made of space.

Experience that the space itself is doing the seeing. You do not have to look in order to see. The seeing happens by itself. You are receiving the visual images without any effort.

Now experience that everything you hear and everything you see occurs at the same time in the space of fundamental consciousness without your making any effort to listen or look. Receive the sounds and the visuals at the same time.

PRACTICE Vision

Here are two practices to help you experience the visual aspect of perceiving as fundamental consciousness.

Sit in front of an object. A living object, like a plant or tree, is preferable, but you can do this with any object.

Inhabit your whole body.

Attune to the space pervading your body and the object.

See if you can experience the space pervading both you and the object so that the object appears to be permeable, pervaded by space. The space pervades and reveals the object. Do not strain for this, but also, do not blur your gaze. Just sit for a few minutes each day (consistency of practice is more effective than the length of each practice session) attuning to the space pervading you and the object. With practice, you will experience the mutual permeability of yourself and the object. If the object is alive, the pervasive space will reveal not only the form, color, and texture of the object but also the life force within it.

Now sit in front of a moving object, such as a flickering candle flame or steam rising from boiling water.

Inhabit your whole body and attune to the space pervading your body and the moving object.

Allow the space to pervade and reveal the moving object.

Let yourself experience the stillness of fundamental consciousness pervading the movement of the object. The flame or the steam moves through the stillness of the space without altering the stillness in any way.

After these visual practices, it is good to rub your hands together in order to make a little heat and then cup your hands (do not press) over your eyes and let your eyes relax by gently absorbing the heat and darkness.

PRACTICE Hearing

Here is a practice to help you experience the hearing aspect of perceiving as fundamental consciousness.

Put some music on, something that you enjoy.

Inhabit your whole body. Find the space outside of your body. Experience that the space inside and outside of your body is the same continuous space. Attune to the space pervading your body and environment.

Let the sound of the music occur in the space without disturbing the stillness of the space. Let yourself experience the stillness of fundamental consciousness and the sound of the music at the same time.

You may even experience that the music is inside and outside of your body at the same time.

Now turn off the music.

Continue to experience that you inhabit your body and the space of fundamental consciousness pervading your body and environment.

Let yourself receive whatever sounds are in your environment in the same way that you received the sound of the music. The sounds in your environment occur in the stillness of FC, without changing the stillness.

PRACTICE Touch

Here is a practice to help you experience the tactile aspect of perceiving as fundamental consciousness.

Inhabit your whole body. Find the space outside of your body. Experience that the space inside and outside of your body is the same continuous space. Attune to the space pervading your body and environment.

Put your hand on an object so you are touching it with your whole hand. Inhabit your hand, as well as the rest of your body, as you do this.

Remaining within your whole body, receive the feel of the object with your whole being.

PRACTICE   Perception of Another Person

A note of caution: All experience is subjective, even when we have realized fundamental consciousness, and subject to our own projections, interpretations, and perceptual limitations. When I teach this exercise in workshops, I always request a firm promise from the participants that they will not share what they see-feel with the person they are observing or with anyone else. I suggest that if you practice this with a partner, you may also want to keep your observations to yourself. This practice is just for the cultivation of your own sensitivity.

Sit facing your partner with your eyes open. Your partner should keep their eyes closed.

Feel that you are inside your whole body. Find the space outside your body. Experience that the space inside and outside of your body is the same continuous space. Experience that the space that pervades you also pervades your partner.

Bring your focus to the space that pervades your partner's head. Allow the space to see-feel inside your partner's head. Do not project your vision into your partner's head but attune to fundamental consciousness already pervading your partner's head. You may be able to see the quality of their being, of their intelligence inside their head. You may be able to see where they are present in their face and head and where they are not present (their pattern of openness and defense). You may also be able to see specific emotions bound in their head and face and the quality of the age that they were when they bound the emotions. You may be able to see-feel what it is like to be that person inside their head.

Then repeat the exercise, bringing your focus to the space pervading your partner's chest. Allow the space to see-feel inside your partner's chest. Do not project your vision into your partner's chest but attune to fundamental consciousness already pervading your partner's chest. You may be able to see the quality of their being, of their emotional life inside their chest. You may be able to see where they are present in their chest and where they are not present (their pattern of openness and defense). You may also be able to see specific emotions bound in their chest and the quality of the age or ages that they were when they bound the emotions. You may be able to see-feel what it is like to be that person inside their chest.

Attune to the space pervading you and your partner's whole body. Allow the space to see-feel your partner within their body. Let yourself see where they live in themselves, where they are more open, and where they are not as open. Let yourself see any emotions held in their body and the age or ages that they were when they bound those emotions. Let yourself see-feel what it is like to be that person inside their body.

Close your eyes. Feel that you are inside your whole body at once. Make deep contact with your own body.

Partners change roles. The person who has had their eyes closed opens them and repeats the practice.

Conclusion

There is another Buddhist story involving the senses that is at the heart of that spiritual tradition because it is about the Buddha's enlightenment. It is said that the Buddha sat in meditation beneath a bodhi tree all night (and probably for years before that) determined to penetrate the mystery of the universe and of his own nature. At dawn, he opened his eyes and saw the morning star. At that moment, he attained enlightenment. He cried out, "I am awakened together with the whole of the great earth and all its beings."

As we release the bound constrictions from our senses, the impact of our sensory experience can be a gateway to the unified spacious ground of our being and of all being. We perceive, with our open senses, that all of life emerges out of and even appears to be made of this same undivided fundamental consciousness as our own self.

7

RELATIONSHIPS
ONENESS AND SEPARATENESS

> Dissociation, as a state of being divided and
> as a chronic process, is ultimately a barrier to
> relationality, both within and between selves.
> ELIZABETH F. HOWELL

Attunement to fundamental consciousness has been considered, until very recently, to be an advanced stage of spiritual realization. We find it described mainly in Asian spiritual texts meant originally for monks. For this reason, some of its characteristics that greatly impact the quality of our daily lives, and especially our relationships, have been ignored. A prime example of this is that fundamental consciousness is a dimension of contact. When we know ourselves and our surroundings as pervaded by fundamental consciousness, we have a sense of being in direct contact with ourselves and everything around us.

Fundamental Consciousness and Contact

Contact is difficult to describe, yet we have all experienced it to some extent. It is a tangible "feel" of connectedness. When you hold someone's hand, for example, you may experience something more than simply the texture of that person's skin or the solidity of their body within your grasp. You may feel a sense of touching and being touched by the person, rather than just the person's body. When you look into someone's eyes, you may experience more than the color and shape of the person's eyes, or even more than their emotional expression. You may feel connection with the person who is looking back at you, as described by the expression "eye contact." It is this mysterious knowing that deepens when we realize fundamental consciousness, as if any obstruction in that basic capacity has been removed.

As fundamental consciousness, we experience that we are made of the same "stuff," the same one consciousness as every thing and everyone that we encounter. This means that our contact with our surroundings is not just from the surface of ourselves with the surface of other objects and beings, but a connection all the way through our own internal depth with the internal depth of everything around us. The internal space of our body, pervaded by fundamental consciousness, has the little-known capacity to contact and know the internal space of other bodies.

This contact does not even require physical touch. We can experience this in-depth contact across distance. We can look at a bird sitting on a branch across a meadow and feel contact with that bird, a resonant connection of our being with the being of the bird. This contact also provides a subtle knowing. It is not a knowing of facts about the bird, in this example, but a knowing of that particular bird's being, the feel of the life within its body. We can pass another human being on the street and experience contact with that person, the resonant connection of our shared aliveness, even if that person is not aware of us. And we can, to some extent, know the feeling of that person's life within their body; the quality of their love, their intelligence, their sexuality; and what it feels like to be that person. This is an intimate knowing of the other person. Yet it is not experienced as intrusive by the other person, because we have not left our own body. In fact, we have to stay connected to our own internal space in order to connect in this deep way. It is just the intrinsic intimacy of fundamental consciousness, pervading our own body and our environment at the same time.

Contact is not necessarily mutual. We can sit in a field or on a bus and experience contact with all of the life around us. This ongoing experience of contact gives us a sense of deep kinship with everyone we encounter and a sense of belonging in our world. It can help us surmount our fears of other people, as well as erode our prejudices and aversions.

For contact to be mutual, both people (or animals) need to inhabit their body. Many of us have touched a dog or cat and felt some answering response of contact from the animal. This mutual contact is even stronger with a human being who inhabits their body, as humans are more conscious than dogs and cats. When two people are both attuned to fundamental consciousness, they experience rich mutual contact throughout the whole internal depth of their bodies.

This is easier to experience than to grasp intellectually. If there is someone nearby as you read this, take a moment to approach them, if possible, and take their hand with your own hand. Now, both of you, inhabit your own hand. You may be able to feel that just by both of you inhabiting the internal space of your own hand, a rich mutual contact occurs. There is a depth of contact throughout the whole internal space of both your hands. And this occurs without any effort to "make contact" with the other person. It occurs just by you each inhabiting your own hand.

This occurs with any part of our body. When you are lying next to someone you know intimately, see if you can experience this with your whole body. Each of you inhabit your own body, as you touch each other, body to body. It is interesting that we experience more contact with each other if we do not merge with each other, if we do not lose contact with ourselves in order to be close to someone else. Instead, we need to remain in contact with ourselves in order to actually experience oneness with another person.

This same whole body to whole body contact can occur across distance. And it can occur with anyone who is also attuned to fundamental consciousness. When two people meet who are both living within the internal space of their body, the qualities that seem to be inherent within their body naturally (spontaneously) resonate with the same qualities within the body of the other person. The love within our own chest, for example, resonates with the love within another person's chest. The quality of our intelligence resonates with the quality of intelligence within another person's head. We can experience this as a true meeting of hearts and minds, even when we are disagreeing with the other person. The resonance of qualities body to body is an important aspect of the richness of our mutual contact with another person. This mutual resonance also stimulates or gently intensifies the qualities for both people.

Fundamental consciousness also reveals our actual boundaries. When two people meet at this ground, they each experience it as the basis of their own sense of existing as an individual at the same time as they experience oneness with each other. This means that they feel both separate from and unified with the other person, at the same time. Our inward contact with the internal space of our body is our demarcation within space and allows us to feel separate from the other person even as we experience oneness with them.

It is interesting that the same ground of fundamental consciousness feels, to each of us, like the basis of our own individual being. An ancient Indian text described this as, "It is one and the same Self that shines as one's own self as well as the selves of others."[1] The eleventh-century Indian philosopher Abhinavagupta wrote, "When the heart is in a state of contraction the awakened awareness of the individual self is in fact a state of ignorance. But when this contraction ceases to function, then the true nature of the Self shines forth."[2]

The Link Between Contact and Trauma

From our earliest moments of life, we develop in relation to other human beings. We learn who we are and who they are, and what the world is like, through our interactions with our primary caretakers and our closest family members. If our early relationships are loving, stable, nurturing, and supportive, we grow up expecting to feel loved, cared for, and supported by other people.

Our traumas occur mainly as ruptures in our early relationships, as failures of love and betrayals of trust. These relational traumas in our childhood may limit our ability to form satisfying relationships as adults. It follows that as we heal the effects of relational trauma, we not only become increasingly whole within our individual selves, we also become more capable of meaningful, authentic relationships with others. We do not need to be in an intimate relationship in order to heal from relational trauma. But healing these ruptures in our early relationships can help us relate more deeply, clearly, and openly with intimate partners and with all of the people in our lives.

Our earliest relationship with our mother, or primary caretaker, affects whether or not we will be able to feel safely and securely connected with another human being later in our life. If our mother is either severely neglectful or abusive, we may avoid intimate relationships as adults. If she is unpredictable in her affection or attention, we may feel a deeply rooted distrust for other people and unable to rely on another person's love.

The mother-child relationship and the ways in which we each cope with the challenges of that relationship are extremely varied and complex. Children bring extraordinary ingenuity to the hard work of protecting and maturing their capacity for love. I knew a woman whose mother was mentally ill and incapable of nurturing her. She had no father or other relatives. As a young child, instead of bonding with her mother, she bonded with a particular tree in her backyard. It may be that her attempt to draw even the slightest amount of warmth from her mother had fine-tuned her ability to receive the unguarded life-force emanating from the tree, or perhaps she was imagining it, but she felt cared for by the tree. She felt that the contact was mutual. She managed to keep her heart open through the sustenance of this communion. She often brought her unresponsive mother wildflowers from the backyard in a gesture that she felt shared with her mother the mothering that she received from the tree. She grew up to be a particularly warm, sane, nurturing wife, mother, and psychotherapist.

It is more likely, though, that we will constrict our ability to bond (to connect deeply and lastingly) with others if we do not experience secure connection with someone early in life. As with all of our trauma-based limitations, the inability to bond involves an actual closing up of an aspect of our body and being.

A woman came to work with me who embodied the effects of this early lack of contact. Sharon was a successful business woman in her fifties. She emanated a quality of no-nonsense competence and independence. She had lived alone for all of her adult life and had never had an intimate relationship. She was a little lonely and had attempted a few relationships over the years but always ended them within a few weeks.

Sharon described her childhood environment as generally happy and loving. However, she was the middle child of a large family, and the many demands on her parents meant that she had mostly raised herself. She described both of her parents in glowing terms, and yet there was no glow of warmth in her demeanor as she spoke of them. A new baby was born when Sharon was barely able to stand, and there were several others already toddling around. I had the impression that Sharon mostly watched this "wonderful mother" from afar, without actually taking her in, without ever feeling close to her.

Sharon told me that she had never had a long-term intimate relationship because she had never met anyone who was good enough for her. "Good enough in what way?" I asked. She did not have to think very long before she answered, "Well, he definitely has to make at least as much money as I do. He needs to be tall and well built. Of course, he should be kind, gentle, not an alcoholic. I prefer dark hair, and I don't like men who are bald. He needs to be very articulate and well-read. And outgoing, not an introvert." These requirements seemed somewhat superficial to me, but more than that, they seemed cold, and it took me a moment to understand why. They seemed like requirements out of a book: the tall, dark, gentle, wealthy man with a full head of hair. They did not take into account the actual experience of attraction, of love.

As Sharon and I continued to talk about this, it occurred to me that she had shut down her ability to experience the pull of attraction, the inexplicable melting of the heart, the spontaneous upwelling of excitement that we feel with some people more than with others. Once we feel this pull, we can certainly reason with ourselves if the person we are attracted to is for some reason inappropriate or unavailable. But if we have shut down the ability to feel it, if we have constricted the spontaneous movement of attraction within our body, we lose our main guidance system for finding someone we love.

I am not saying that intimate relationships are necessary for happiness. There are so many sources of happiness in life, and no one can judge what is best for someone else. But to constrict our ability to bond is not the same as making a life choice of unencumbered solitude. To shut down any part of ourselves limits our whole being and to some extent, diminishes our capacity for any kind of happiness.

One day in our session together, Sharon was focusing within the tension in her upper chest, and she felt sadness there. As she began to release the tension, she realized that it was not really sadness; it was longing. Then she remembered standing across the room from her mother, as her mother struggled, none too gently, to diaper a young infant. She said, "The baby, my brother Ben, was crying and flailing his arms around. She tried to hold him down with one hand while arranging the diaper with the other, and she seemed angry. I had fallen and scraped my hand; I can remember how it stung. I wanted her to look over at me, even to hold me, but I knew that she wouldn't. I don't remember ever wanting her to hold me after that." As she pictured her mother, she could feel the movement within her upper chest, as it closed against the feeling of longing and then released. She said, "Oh, it feels like there is more space in there for me." Then, suddenly, she smiled. The face of a friend of hers had appeared in her mind, and, for the first time that she could remember, she felt a "surge of love" in her chest.

When we heal and release the trauma-based constrictions in our body, we become more capable of experiencing attraction, desire, and love for others. We are also able to feel that we are entitled to have that desire and love reciprocated. Also, our contact with ourselves helps us to tolerate and accept the otherness of other people without feeling threatened or displaced by their differences from ourselves. We are able to "hang in" through difficulties in relationships so they develop over time and may even become lifelong bonds with friends and intimate partners.

Balancing Inward and Outward Connection

There has been an interesting shift in the past few decades in much of the psychotherapy field regarding the goal of psychological healing and maturity. The older schools of psychotherapy claim that individuation, the ability to know and experience oneself as a separate individual, is the goal, while many of the newer schools point to relational health, the ability to form and maintain satisfying relationships, as the endpoint. This shift reflects a general new wave of understanding in our culture of the ways in which human beings and all of nature can be seen as an interdependent system, even a field of mutual influence in which the individual is inextricably embedded. This post-modern Western idea that there really is no separate autonomous self and for that matter, no objective reality that can be separated from the subjectivity of the observer, fits very well with some Asian concepts of interdependence and nonduality.

However, since these two perspectives (emphasizing individuation and interdependence) rarely take the body into account, they both often go too far in their theories. When we experience fundamental consciousness pervading our body and environment as unity, we see that individuation is an integral part of nonduality. As FC, we mature as a separate person, at the same time as we transcend our separateness. We can only connect with our environment to the extent that we have inward connection with ourselves. Wherever we inhabit the internal space of our body, we are open and responsive to our surroundings. Interdependence does not eradicate individuation, and individuation does not eradicate interdependence.

In the 1950s, Margaret Mahler, one of the first innovators in the field of child development, developed a theory called "separation-individuation."[3] She claimed that we begin life psychologically merged with our mother. We do not make any distinction between her experience and our own. Gradually, over the first three years of life (in Mahler's optimistic opinion), we individuate from our mother and know ourselves as a separate person. In the eighties, Daniel Stern's research showed that children do have a rudimentary sense of separation; they can distinguish themselves from their mother, even as new born infants.[4] But he agreed with Mahler that this ability matures over time. He added the important insight that along with the maturing of individuation comes the maturing of our ability for intimacy with another person. As we know our own subjectivity, we have the ability to recognize and relate to the separate subjectivity of another person.

As children, our pathway of development is to deepen contact with both ourselves and others. If we do not meet with much adversity, this dual line of inward and outward contact occurs simultaneously. The more inward contact we have with ourselves, the more available we are for contact with others. We can speculate that this would be a natural, spontaneous process, a kind of inward ripening toward the subtle core of the body and simultaneously, toward our realization of self and other as fundamental consciousness if it were not for the patterns of constriction that we all mirror and develop as children. These constrictions prevent us from fully inhabiting our body and from arriving at the core of our being. We get used to living on or near the surface of ourselves rather than in the internal depth of ourselves. We get used to being, to some extent, limited in our contact with other people. This is our common human condition.

Often children need to choose between the two sides of maturation: inward contact with themselves and connection with others. If our parents' affection seems stifling or intrusive, we may shut down our capacity for contact with others in an attempt to protect the integrity and autonomy of our individual being. Or, in response to this intrusive love, or if our parents are emotionally distant, we may abandon inward contact with ourselves and pursue closeness with our family by becoming merged and enmeshed with them. However, both of these patterns results in a constriction of our ability to truly connect both with ourselves and with others.

These two types of relating—shutting people out or self-abandonment and merging with others—may continue to be our way of relating in our adult lives. Both relational patterns diminish our ability to love and to receive love. Both patterns shut down, to some extent, our inward access to our own thoughts, emotions, and sensations. Both patterns limit our capacity to truly see and know another person, to respond emotionally to them, and to experience genuine arousal and pleasure in our physical contact with them.

There has been much research done on early attachment patterns with our mother and how those patterns affect our later relationships. But our ways of relating continue to form throughout the early years of our childhood and even throughout our adolescence. Our relationships with our parents, siblings, and extended family; with authority figures; and with our peers all contribute to our implicit patterns of relating. They affect whether we meet others with openness or with suspicion, with trust or with fear. They influence whether we feel comfortable as we walk through our world or whether we feel overly conspicuous and self-conscious or invisible. And they affect whether we build a fortress around ourselves that deprives us of human warmth or whether we ignore our own needs and preferences to lose ourselves in relationships with others.

Psychologists agree that secure attachment involves the ability to be both intimate and separate. Margaret Mahler described the pinnacle of relational maturity as "object constancy"—the ability to be secure enough in our attachments that we can endure separation from our beloved and welcome them when they return.[5] If attachment is not secure, the child (and immature adult) will slide into hopeless despair during a separation. The return of the beloved will be met with wariness, resentment, and distrust. The broken heart will not risk further injury. The healthy, resilient heart, however, will continue to love even during times of separation. But in order to be resilient to separation and loss, we need to be able to be alone without feeling abandoned. We need to have enough internal connection with ourselves that we can enjoy our senses and our own thoughts and creativity, when we are alone, and yet be open enough to other people to enjoy their company when we are not alone.

Most of us can be described as introverted or extroverted. These are normal personality preferences. They are only problematic if our bodily organizations of protection and compensation prevent us from having flexibility in our ability to be alone or with others.

PRACTICE   Attuning to the Qualities Within the Body with a Partner

Sit facing the other person, each of you on a chair, with your feet on the floor, and your eyes open. Both partners follow these instructions at the same time.

Feel that you are inside your whole body at once. Find the space outside of you. Experience that the space inside and outside your body is the same, continuous space. It pervades you. Experience that the space that pervades your body also pervades your partner. Remain in your own body as you experience this.

You do not need to maintain eye contact throughout this exercise, but keep your eyes open so you are aware of your partner visually.

Feel that you are inside your whole brain. Find the space inside your own brain and inside your partner's brain at the same time.

Attune to the quality of understanding inside your brain. Attune to your own quality of understanding and your partner's quality of understanding at the same time.

Feel that you are inside your neck. Find the space inside your own neck and inside your partner's neck at the same time.

Attune to the quality of your voice inside your neck. Attune to your own quality of voice and your partner's quality of voice at the same time.

Feel that you are inside your chest. Let yourself settle in your chest so you feel like you are sitting in your heart. Find the space inside your own chest and inside your partner's chest at the same time.

Attune to the quality of love inside your chest. Attune to your own quality of love and your partner's quality of love at the same time.

Feel that you are inside your midsection. Find the space inside your own midsection and inside your partner's midsection at the same time.

Attune to the quality of power inside your midsection. Attune to your own quality of power and your partner's quality of power at the same time.

Feel that you are inside your pelvis. Find the space inside your own pelvis and inside your partner's pelvis at the same time.

Attune to the quality of gender, however that feels to you, inside your pelvis. Attune to your own quality of gender and your partner's quality of gender at the same time.

Feel that you are inside your whole body at once. Attune to the quality of self inside your whole body. Attune to your own quality of self and your partner's quality of self at the same time.

Find the space outside your body. Experience that the space inside and outside your body is the same continuous space. Feel that the space that pervades you also pervades your partner.

As that space, you can let go of your grasp on both yourself and your partner. Let yourself and your partner be just as you are in this moment. Let the space pervade and receive you both.

Healing Our Capacity for Contact

In the past decade, the diagnosis of autism has been expanded to include a spectrum of behavioral patterns. Now, anyone who has some difficulty bonding, expressing emotion, or communicating with other people is often characterized as "on the spectrum." Whereas autism is a severe and still little-understood disorder, there can be many reasons for more common degrees of difficulty in relating. And while the popular notion of being "on the autism spectrum" has brought more acceptance to introverted behavior and more appreciation for the diversity of relational styles, it has also caused some damage. People who could overcome their barriers to love may be labeled as somehow innately hermetic and considered to be irreparably limited. If we understand how trauma causes us to organize our whole organism, we will see that much of what has been labeled "on the spectrum" can be healed.

When Martha first came to work with me, she was extremely introverted. Sitting opposite her in my office, I was most aware of how still she was holding herself. So I was not very surprised when she said that she had sought me out because she was interested in my teaching of the "pervasive stillness." But the pervasive stillness of fundamental consciousness is not the same as holding oneself still. It is the antithesis of holding oneself still. "Good," I said. "I think that attuning to that pervasive stillness may be very helpful for you."

I asked her if she had an intimate partner, and she gave a dismissive laugh. But at the same time, there was a slight movement in her chest.

"Are you lonely?" I asked. "Not really," she said. "I had a boyfriend in high school but not in the past twenty years. I'm not interested in that any more. My work keeps me very busy." There was a long silence, in which she became even stiller, watching me carefully, but without expression.

After several moments, I asked, "What are you thinking?" "Nothing." "Nothing? So what were you doing?" She introspected for a moment and then, with a little embarrassment, she said, "I was saying a mantra."

"Do you do that a lot?" I asked. "Mantra repetition?"

"I guess so. Not when I'm alone so much. When I'm with other people."

"You say the mantra in social situations?"

"Yes. It passes the time," she said, with a slightly inward smile, as if sharing a joke with herself. "I guess it makes me less nervous." There was another silence, and suddenly I saw a look of recognition in her eyes. She had had an insight or a memory. "What is it?" I asked.

"I just remembered something." Then, haltingly, she began to tell me about her childhood. Over the next few weeks, we both began to gain some insight into her pattern of "keeping her mind occupied" in social situations.

Her father, who she vaguely remembered as a quiet, gentle man, died when she was four. That left her alone with her mother. She was a bitter, furious, alcoholic woman, "a walking time bomb" who would explode unpredictably at Martha, "screaming and cursing." She called her "ugly" and "stupid" and "weak as your father was," only increasing in volume and cruelty if Martha turned away from her. Martha learned that she could withstand her mother's attacks if she held very still and filled her head with "white noise" by humming or repeating words silently to herself. She also hardened herself inside her body so she would not feel anything toward her mother, even when her mother broke down crying in drunken self-pity and begged for her forgiveness. She had not been aware until she began to explain this to me that this holding still and even the humming had become a chronic pattern that began in her childhood.

Martha also recognized that the way she was practicing meditation was augmenting this stillness. She sat with a Zen teacher several times a week who demanded absolute stillness in his students. "He yells if we move," Martha said.

Sitting still can help us find and cultivate the internal movement of energy in our body. But, if misunderstood, it can have the opposite effect, causing the student to hold even their internal movement still and to become increasingly rigid.

Martha and I worked for about a year, helping her to inhabit her body and to attune to the space of fundamental consciousness pervading her body and environment. With practice, she was able to experience that, instead of holding herself still, the pervasive space was naturally still. But even this natural stillness was not the kind of blankness that we experience when we hold ourselves still. Instead, it feels alive and vibrant. And our breath, which we usually hold when we hold ourselves still, moves freely through the space, enlivening our whole body.

Maintaining her attunement to fundamental consciousness when there was another person nearby continued to be challenging for Martha. It was in relation to her mother that she had learned to shut down, to close up, and she automatically returned to that pattern in her encounters with other human beings. She particularly shut down her sexuality and her love. She tightened her pelvis and her chest in the same way that she had shielded herself against her mother's toxic emotions and against feeling her own responses of terror, loss, and anger toward her.

One day I sat facing Martha, a little closer to her than I usually sat when we worked together. Although we had known each other for some time, and Martha had come to trust that I would not be in any way cruel toward her, she still held still within her chest as soon as I sat down right in front of her. I led her through the partner exercise described above. "Feel that you are in your head," I said. She was used to this instruction and easily inhabited her head. I continued, "And I am over here inhabiting my head. Now let's both find the space inside our own head and inside each other's head at the same time. At first Martha came forward in her head, as if to meet me. I asked her to stay deeply within her head as she also found the space inside my head.

This "finding" is difficult to put into words, but most everyone that I have worked with has been able to do it. It is not a visual finding, not a looking within the other person's body, but rather a connecting from within the internal space of one's own body to the internal space of the other person's body. We need to be situated deeply within our own body in order to do this.

When Martha moved back into the internal depth of her head, there was automatically contact of the internal space of her head with the internal space of my own head. This contact feels like a matching vibration, a very gentle, simultaneous "buzz" within each of our heads.

We smiled at each other. This connection is so satisfying, it feels as if this deep contact or oneness is one of our fundamental, but rarely met, needs. One of my students likened it to when one is turning a dial on a radio, trying to find a specific radio station but at first encounters static and then finally lands right on the station, and it can be clearly heard. That landing right on the station is like what happens when two people find this attunement to each other from within the internal space of their bodies.

"Now attune to the quality of your understanding inside your head." Martha could also do this easily. "And attune to your own quality of understanding and mine at the same time." This produced the same connection as before, when we were connecting "inner space to inner space" but was further enlivened by the addition of the quality of understanding.

We repeated this attunement exercise with our throat and the quality of voice within our throat, again finding that satisfying connection.

Then we came to the chest. Martha anticipated this by shutting down a little more forcefully. "Do you want to try this?" I asked. "Let's do it," she said, bracing herself a little harder.

"Okay. Feel that you are inside your chest. And I'm going to be over here, inhabiting my own chest." Most children, because they are relatively undefended, feel barraged and penetrated by the emotions of adults, especially when anger is directed toward them. That is why I assured Martha that I would be "over here" in my own body, inhabiting my own chest—not coming out toward her.

I said, "Now, staying within our own chest, let's both find the space within our own chest and each other's chest at the same time." Although a little tentative, Martha was able to do this, and we felt some connection between us.

"Now let's each attune to the quality of love within our own chest," I said.

It is important for people to feel that they can attune to love within their own chest, even without connecting with another person. This is one's own love; it belongs to us and to no one else—feeling love within our own body does not obligate us to be loving toward anyone else.

When Martha was able to feel her own love in her chest, I continued, "Now let's both find the love in our chest and in each other's chest at the same time."

When Martha and I did this, we immediately felt the contact of her love and mine, and at the same time, a huge wave of love moved through her. We often speak of "waves" of emotion, and this was really like a wave, like a huge ocean wave that moved through her whole chest as if suddenly breaking through its bonds.

For a moment, Martha looked afraid, and then she seemed to realize that this wave could move through her without overwhelming her, that it could break through its barriers without breaking her. She looked over at me, a little embarrassed at first, and then she laughed and laughed as she allowed this new warmth to move through her.

PRACTICE Core-to-Core Attunement with a Partner

This is a practice for connecting with another person from the subtle core of one's body. Just as in the previous practice of connecting with another person from within the internal space and the internal qualities of one's body, this core-to-core attunement can help us experience both oneness and distance from another person at the same time.

Sit facing a friend, each of you on a chair, with your feet on the floor and your eyes open. Both partners follow these instructions at the same time.

Find the center of your head. Now make eye contact with each other across the distance; be aware of the distance between you. From the center of your head, find the center of your partner's head. Do not leave your own head to do this.

Find your heart center. Staying in your heart center, make eye contact with each other, while aware of the distance between you. From your heart center, find your partner's heart center. Be careful not to come out of your own heart center to do this.

Find your pelvic center. Staying in your pelvic center, make eye contact with each other, while aware of the distance between you. From your own pelvic center, find your partner's pelvic center.

Now attune to each other with all three points: Find the center of your head again. Find the center of your head and your heart center at the same time. Find the center of your head, your heart center, and your pelvic center at the same time. Staying in all three points, make eye contact with each other, while aware of the distance between you. From all three points in your own body, find the same three points in your partner's body.

This exercise can be done with any of the chakras, including the one above the head.

Healing Our Capacity for Contact from Our Core

At the other extreme from someone who has withdrawn and shielded themselves from contact with others is the person who abandons contact with themselves and comes forward energetically to merge with another person. People with this pattern are often experienced as invasive. Their relational style may be exacerbated because the person they are trying to relate with may draw back or protect themselves against this intrusion. This may cause the person who is attempting to merge to try even harder, to come out of their own body even further toward the other person, in their pursuit of connection.

When Serena came to work with me, I had to resist the impulse to move my chair further away from her. I felt almost smothered by her, even though we were seated several feet away from each other. At the same time, her body seemed almost hollow, as if she had barely any contact with herself. Just as Martha's Zen practice had augmented her protective pattern of holding herself still, Serena's spiritual teacher had emphasized that no one really exists. Serena told me with some pride that she had never felt she existed.

Over the next few months, Serena practiced inhabiting her body. She was able to recognize how she came out of her body in order to connect with her environment, but it was a life-long pattern and took some time to change. It helped her inhabit her body when she could feel that the container of her body had a front. She was used to "falling out" of the front of herself, as if there were nothing there to contain her. But by inhabiting her skin, she began to have a tangible sense of a container that she could reside within. This envelope of the body is both permeable and tangible at the same time.

Serena described often feeling smothered by her mother. "All the women in my family are smushed together," she said. "It's their way of loving." Naturally, she had mirrored her mother's relational style since she was an infant. She said that she had always felt a little guilty that she did not really feel loved by her mother, even though her mother had always been so affectionate toward her. It had felt like they never truly connected with each other. "She loves me, but she doesn't really know me," she said.

The practice of the core-to-core attunement was the most helpful of the Realization Process practices for her. At first, she was very hesitant even to try the practice. She was afraid that if she stayed within the core of her body, she would be isolated. When she found the center of her head, she said, "I'm too far away from you." It also became clear, to both of us, that in remaining in her own core while relating to another person, she was breaking a family taboo. "Are you sure this is okay?" she asked, and then laughed at her own question.

When she finally allowed herself to find my heart center, while remaining in her own heart center, she was so amazed that she began to cry. She had not expected to be able to feel the resonance of love with another person while remaining within the innermost core of herself. She described it as, "I'm alone, but I'm also with you."

Part of the core to core attunement practice is to make eye contact with one's partner, while aware of the distance between you. This was particularly important for Serena. The eyes are an important medium of contact, and that may be why they are so often involved in our defenses against contact. We use the eyes to shut people out, hardening them like shields. And we also use the eyes to merge with other people or to pull people toward us.

Serena said that she had always been uncomfortable with eye contact because it seemed "fuzzy" to her. But when she looked in my eyes while aware of the distance between us, the space suddenly seemed to elongate between us. We both felt further away from each other spatially but more connected with each other. This was our true distance from each other. By "true" I mean that we were not manipulating our focus to push each other away or pull each other closer. It allowed us to look in each other's eyes with a clear sense of mutual contact.

Healing Intimate Relationships

Contact between people is visible to the sensitive eye. I like to work with couples seated on a couch because how they place themselves on the couch can reveal so much about their relationship and also how it may change over the course of the therapy. But even more important than how close or far from each other they place themselves is how much contact radiates between them. The contact between them shows how open they are to each other, how deeply they receive each other's presence, and how much resonance occurs between them, even if they are not conscious of it. When people are open to each other they will feel both relaxed and enlivened by each other.

Most couples are more open to each other in some parts of themselves than in other parts. This is because of our design of openness and constriction. Wherever we inhabit our own body, we can experience contact with another person who inhabits that same part of their body. Part of what draws people to each other is this shared openness and the depth of contact that it creates between them. But we also seem to be drawn to people who are not open where we are, partly out of admiration for qualities that we do not possess as fully and also perhaps as a way of becoming more whole. However, these differences, which were at first attractive, can become the deepest conflicts within a relationship. They need to be resolved, and both partners need to become more fully open to each other if the relationship is to survive and grow.

A couple may report that what they love most about their relationship is the lively exchange of ideas, the stimulating conversation. They enjoy their meeting of minds. Another couple may say that their relationship is really about sex, that if not for their "great sex," they would probably not be together. And other couples may feel a depth of love with each other that keeps them warm and close even if they feel compelled to seek out others for conversation or for sex. But often this limitation in a couple's contact with each other becomes problematic for them, and they may bring this problem into therapy. It can be frustrating for them that they connect so well in some ways and not in others. They may not want to give up the type of contact that they do feel with their partner, even when the lack of contact between them in other areas—sexually, emotionally, or intellectually—has become intolerable.

Of course, opening to each other throughout the whole body and experiencing contact in all aspects of themselves rather than just in one aspect does not necessarily mean that the relationship will work. People may both inhabit their heads and be able to experience resonance with each other in the quality of their intelligence and still not have similar enough interests to enjoy conversation with each other. They may be able to feel the resonance of love with each other within their chests and still not actually love each other. We can feel this emotional resonance with anyone, even a stranger that we pass momentarily on the street. But what makes us love a particular person is more mysterious and involves many more factors than contact.

However, if people do love each other, but the constrictions in their body prevent them from fully feeling, receiving, and expressing this love, then inhabiting the internal space of their chests and experiencing emotional resonance with each other can help deepen and heal their connection. If two people are interested in each other's mind, but old patterns in either or both partners blocks the expression of themselves intellectually, then inhabiting the internal space of their heads and experiencing actual mind-to-mind oneness and resonance can help dissolve these barriers. Inhabiting the pelvis and genital area and experiencing resonance with each other in the qualities of gender and sexuality can almost always help resolve sexual difficulties between two people who want to be together.

When I work with couples, in addition to providing a place where they can both speak and actually hear and respond to each other, I also teach them the relational practices described in this chapter. These practices, attuning to the resonance of the qualities within their bodies and attuning core-to-core with each other, reveal clearly where people are able to connect with each other. They also help both partners recognize how they are blocking the contact between them and why. Over time, the act of attuning to each other from within their bodies can also help dissolve the blockages of contact between them.

It has often been said that we recreate our conflicts with our parents or their conflicts with each other in our present relationships. We may feel that we have chosen someone who is exactly the opposite of our mother or father, and then, just a few months into the relationship, we find ourselves in exactly the same predicament as when we were children. This latent conflict seems to be one of the factors in our attraction to an intimate partner. Harville Hendrix, who developed the Imago method of healing relationships, claimed that this is part of our innate impulse toward healing and wholeness. Recently I worked with a couple who were a good illustration of how our constrictions can match those of our partner to bring childhood trauma to the surface.

When I first met Janice and Lenny, they sat on opposite ends of the couch, as far from each other as they could get. But even across that distance, there was some subtle flow of love, permeating the space between them. "I know he's not stupid," Janice said to me, motioning toward the man who was now cringing even further away from her, as she began to speak. "But if I talk about anything, the books I'm reading, the political issues, it's like a shutter comes down. We've been together nine years now, and it's always been like this. Maybe I just bore him, but I can't be with someone any more who is not interested in me."

We both looked over at Lenny to see his response to his. But he acted as if he hadn't heard anything. It really was like a shutter had come down between them. "Is her conversation boring?" I asked.

Lenny looked at the floor for what seemed like a long time, and then shook his head, no. "Of course not," he said.

"Well, then what is it?" Janice demanded. "Even just this morning, I wanted to talk to you about the film we went to last night. I thought it was really moving, but the ending was a little disappointing, wasn't it, and you just got up in the middle of me talking and left the room. You left the room!"

I turned to Lenny. "What do you feel when you hear her speak?" I asked, although I was beginning to have some idea. His head had become progressively narrower as Janice attempted to get through to him. It looked as if he was holding his hands over his ears, but without his hands. I also noticed that Janice had also distorted her head. She seemed to be pushing her forehead toward him as she spoke, as if this might provide more impact to her words.

I worked first with Lenny to see if he could become aware of this movement in his head when Janice spoke. It did not take long for him to be able to focus within the chronic tension on the sides of his head and in his ears, to feel how it moved further into constriction, then to let go of it, and to feel it release slightly. "My head seems to get rounder as I let go," he said.

Then suddenly, he said he felt fear. "What of?" I asked.

"I feel like I'm going to be overwhelmed by her voice. I feel like she's talking at me." He turned toward Janice. "I feel like you're attacking me with your voice. It's not what you're saying. I can't even make out the words. I just hear your tone."

"But that's because you never listen!" she yelled. "Wow," she said, turning to me. "I sound exactly like my mother. Oh, my god, I never heard that before. I'm sorry. I'm so sorry, Lenny." That session ended with them both crying and comforting each other.

The next time we met, they were ready to work on releasing the organizations in both their heads that intensified when they tried to communicate with each other. Janice was able to feel clearly how she mirrored her mother's forehead when she talked to Lenny. "It's like a little spear comes out of the center of it," she said. As she focused on allowing the "spear" to emerge and release, she felt how both she and her mother had tried to penetrate her father's remoteness. "He was like a stone. He'd come home from work exhausted and sit and have one beer after another, and just turn to stone." When she imagined her father, in his chair with his hand wrapped around a beer bottle, she could feel how the tension in her forehead also constricted her voice so everything she said had to be forced almost violently out of her mouth.

"I just need you to listen to me, Lenny," she said.

For his part, Lenny found that when he allowed his head to narrow, blocking his hearing, he remembered how he had done the same exact movement in relation to his father. "He was so condescending," he said. "He just had to know everything. He could never just talk; he had to pontificate."

Both patterns, Lenny's constriction of his head and ears and Janice's jutting forward in her forehead, were formed long before they met each other. Yet the two patterns fit each other perfectly to reenact traumatic situations from both their childhoods. If Lenny did not have this preexisting pattern, he would not have reacted so intensely to Janice's style of communication. And if Janice did not already have her pattern of relating, formed in her childhood, she would not have reacted so intensely to Lenny's difficulty listening. Their matching patterns exacerbated their childhood wounding but also gave both of them a chance to heal this wounding.

Along with the release work, I also led Janice and Lenny in the Realization Process partner practices. As expected, they were able to inhabit their own bodies and connect easily with each other in all areas of themselves except their throats and heads. But as they continued to heal and release their own patterns of constriction, the resonance between them in these areas gradually improved. When they were finally able to remain in their throats and attune to their own quality of voice and each other's at the same time, Janice said, "I never felt before that there was room for my own voice. I can just stay where I am and speak." When she did that, Lenny also relaxed and found that he could receive the sound of her voice, without defending against it, and even listen to what she was saying.

Healing Our Relationships with Groups

Experiencing ourselves as the pervasive space of fundamental consciousness is not only healing for our intimate or other one-on-one relationships. It can also help heal our sense of being both an individual and connected with others in group situations.

Many people feel uncomfortable in groups. They may feel that their individual experience will be obliterated by the presence of so many other people and that their own voice will be "drowned out" by the presence of other voices. Old feelings of alienation, of feeling different from other people and shut out of the general comradery of their peers especially during their schooldays, may be brought to the surface by present-day group situations. The two main Realization Process practices, attunement to fundamental consciousness and the core breath, can be expanded to help people feel more connected to other people within a group without losing their experience of individuality.

In my workshops and teacher trainings I always work individually with each person (who wants to do this) in front of the group. For the people observing the work, it is a way to practice remaining attuned to fundamental consciousness even when intense emotions are being expressed by the person working. There is also a transmission of release, where the observers may experience some release of their own holding patterns and some new openness, as the person in front of the group releases and opens. And there is the reassurance that we are not alone, not at all strange in our suffering. Every one of us has had to navigate the labyrinth of our parents' imperfect human love, the specific lacks in their ability to nurture and connect with us. We are not alone in our experience of grief, terror, and fury; in our basic human needs, no matter how overwhelming they may seem at times; and in our sense of being wounded and incomplete.

One of the greatest obstacles to recovery from trauma is the tendency of all children to blame themselves for whatever happened to them. Several years ago, it became popular to criticize psychotherapy for placing all the blame on one's parents. And it is true that many psychotherapists and many modes of psychotherapy offered no way to overcome the anger toward one's parents once they had helped the client to uncover it. So people became "stuck" in blame. But I think that even the virulence of this blame and resentment that became obsessive for so many psychotherapy clients was often a cover for deeper feelings of self-blame.

It is easy to see that parental abuse is a legacy, a passing down of woundedness from one generation to the next. So most of us, as we become more self-aware, can let our parents off the hook. But it is more challenging to recognize our own innocence—to recognize that we in no way invited the sexual groping from an abusive adult, that whatever childhood mischief we got into did not merit the beating or the boxing of ears, or that our parents' constant disapproval was based not on our own flaws but on their own frustration or jealousy. However, when we regard another human being describing their childhood traumas, we can clearly see their innocence. When we witness another person's release work in front of the group, we can easily understand that they were not at all responsible for their parents' abuse or negligence, and then, we can more easily see our own innocence as well.

It is also healing to be the person working in front of the group. The format in the workshops and teacher trainings is that the person I am working with sits in front of the room, facing the rest of the group. I sit facing the person working with my back to the group. This means that even before our work begins, the person who is about to work is faced with a group of observers, an audience. Some are used to this and take it in stride. Some ignore it, shuttering out all but our one-on-one relationship. But most people must take a moment to adjust to being the center of attention, to having people look at them.

One of the most important shifts that occurs as we inhabit our body is that we become less self-conscious. We all grow up being looked at from our first moments after our birth. The more sensitive we are to the people around us, the more aware we will be of the way people respond to us. Most of us objectify ourselves to some extent—we prepare ourselves to be an object of observation. And most of us worry about how well we rate as an object—how beautiful or intelligent or good or kind we appear to others. We adjust ourselves to our observers to appear in a way that meets with their approval. We create what in popular parlance has been called a "false self," a "personae," or a social mask. But these masks keep slipping; they must be constantly monitored and also adjusted, and this doubting of the effectiveness of our mask contributes to our self-consciousness.

Also, many people have a childhood history of being mis-seen or seen only in a very superficial way. For example, a little girl may be praised by all the adults in her family for her physical attributes. "What a pretty girl you are! Look at those beautiful blue eyes" they might say, without ever seeing or responding to the expression in those eyes. The approval or disapproval that we receive from our parents may be bewildering to us if it does not seem to match our internal experience of ourselves. But we do not yet have enough discernment to choose our own assessment of ourselves over that of our parents'. So we begin to adjust to the way we are seen, abandoning our nascent internal experience of ourselves. This also is an objectification of ourselves—a shift away from subjectivity to objectification. Often when people feel afraid of being seen, they are really afraid that they will be seen inaccurately or only superficially, or unfairly, negatively judged.

One of the most effective ways to overcome self-consciousness is to allow ourselves to be seen. To be transparent, receptive, and present to the gaze of the other person. When we inhabit our body and experience ourselves as the unified ground of our being, we know ourselves as the subject of our experience, rather than as the object of other people's experience. This means that we can receive the gaze of the other person without abandoning ourselves. Our experience of ourselves, based on our actual contact with ourselves, cannot be changed by the people seeing us, by what they think they see or how they respond to what they think they see.

At a recent workshop a woman named Rita made her way hesitantly to the front of the room to work with me. People always have the choice of not participating in this part of the workshop, but most people who come to these workshops have extraordinary courage regarding their personal growth. Although I remind them that it can take as much courage to say no, most choose to make the trip to the chair in front of the group, however fraught the journey is for them. By the time Rita sat down in front of me and the others in the group, she was trembling. First, she shut her eyes tightly, then opened them, and reared back in her chair as if a strong wind was assaulting her from the group.

"You don't have to look at them," I said. "You can look down a little, at the space between us." She lowered her focus but remained rigidly still, her legs tight together and her hands clasped tightly in her lap.

"Feel that you are in your feet," I began. "See if you can experience yourself inside your feet, even though there are those people in front of you." As I led her through the practice of inhabiting the body that we had already done several times in the workshop she began to soften internally, to make contact with herself. "Let yourself experience that you are living inside your whole body at once," I continued. I waited until she was in her whole body and breathing evenly.

"Without even looking at the group and staying within your whole body, let yourself feel that the space that pervades you pervades all of us in this room." Having already practiced this for several days in the workshop, Rita was able to do this. "Now, still staying present within your body, let yourself receive the gazes of everyone here—as warmth. See if you can even feel nourished by this warmth." Keeping her own focus toward the floor between us, Rita opened herself to the human warmth in the room. The feeling of warmth made her smile. "This feels good," she said. But then she looked up at me. "Of course, this feels good here. These people are so sweet. I know I can trust them. But how do I do this out in the world?" I looked behind me, at the compassionate, open faces of the group as they sat huddled together, watching silently.

I continued, "Let yourself feel again that the space of fundamental consciousness that pervades you, pervades everyone here. Now, instead of receiving their gazes, let all of the human vibrations in the room pass through this space without changing it in any way." Rita found that she was able to do this, and to her surprise, she was then able to lift her focus and take in the group visually, without feeling overwhelmed. I said, "This is something you can practice wherever you are—in the supermarket, on a bus, in any group situation. You always have a choice: you can let the vibrations of other people pass through the space or you can receive them and let yourself feel nourished by them."

PRACTICE Attuning to the Core Points in Groups

The following instructions are for the whole group.

Sit upright with your eyes closed and your feet on the floor. Feel that you are inside your whole body at once.

Find the center of your head. From the center of your own head, without leaving the center of your head, find the center of the head of the other people in the room.

Find your heart center in the center of your chest but deep in the core of your body. From your own heart center, without leaving your heart center, find the heart center of the other people in the room.

Find your pelvic center in the center of your pelvis but deep in the core of your body. From your own pelvic center, without leaving your pelvic center, find the pelvic center of the other people in the room.

Find the center of your head, your heart center, and your pelvic center at the same time. From these three points in your own body, find these three points in the other people in the room.

PRACTICE Walking in the City

Walk down a busy city street.

Inhabit your whole body. Find the space outside of your body. Experience that the space inside and outside of your body is the same, continuous space. Experience that the space that pervades you pervades your whole environment, as you walk down the street.

Allow the sights, sounds, and smells of the city street to pass through the space as you walk. Allow the vibrations of the other people to pass through the space as you walk. Remain present within your whole body as you do this.

Alternately, let yourself receive the vibrations of the other people on the street as you walk. Let yourself feel nourished by their human warmth. Remain present within your whole body as you do this.

This can also be practiced in any situation where there are crowds of people.

8

THE REALIZATION PROCESS RELEASE TECHNIQUE

Trauma is responsible for disruptions
in the development of self-reflexivity,
intersubjectivity, and embodiment.

LEWIS ARON

So far, in this book, I have looked at how trauma disrupts and fragments our experience of our internal wholeness, and our openness and connection with our environment. I have defined trauma as any event that is too overwhelming, too painful, or too confusing for us to fully experience and to remain present to with our whole body, heart, and mind. In chapter 1, I described how we constrict our body against the impact of trauma, binding within these constrictions the memories and emotions of the traumatic events. We also constrict our body in order to suppress behaviors, such as crying or expressing anger, that might evoke traumatic encounters with other people. We constrict ourselves in order to mirror the patterns of defense and openness of our parents and to comply with parental demands, such as not to be "so smart" or to be less active or noisy. And we harden ourselves into shapes that compensate for the limitations caused by these constrictions, for example, by jutting out our chest to mimic power when we have constricted and diminished our actual power.

I described how, when repeated over time, these movements into constriction either become well-worn habitual reactions to circumstances that remind us of the traumatic events or even harden into rigid, immovable binding within our body. I also wrote that, even though these movements into constriction are spontaneous and unconscious, there is still an agent of the movement, our own will, along with the feeling of our mentality at the age when we first constricted ourselves, that is also revealed as we release this binding. This means that even though it often feels like the binding in our body has been done to us, it was always we ourselves who did the binding.

In this chapter, I present the Realization Process method for releasing the patterns of constriction from our body. This release technique requires that we are first able inhabit our body and to attune to and live within the subtle core of the body. This enables us to maintain the stability of knowing ourselves in the present moment so when we open ourselves to an experience from our past, we are not overwhelmed by the memories or emotions of the past events. The Realization Process release technique is not a regressive method. We do not become the wounded child that we uncover and release within these holding patterns. We are able to feel the emotions of that child part of ourselves, while still observing them from the vantage point of our present-day contact with the internal space of our body.

The method also requires that we have access to the subtle core of the body because it uses our ability to direct our attention inward with a refined, precise focus. It is based on our ability to connect with the core level of our body, the spark of our fundamental consciousness, within the bound fragments of ourselves.

An important aspect of this release technique is that, as we become free of these constrictions in our body, we are more fully able to inhabit our body. We do not just become more open as we release these patterns; we also gain more inward contact with ourselves and with the innate qualities of our being. Because of this, we do not feel more vulnerable as we let go of our childhood defenses; we feel more unified and present within our body. We gain a richer, more tangible experience of our own existence.

This technique is very simple, but because it works with the exact pathways of our psychological constrictions, it can also be very powerful. Like any deep psychological work, it is most effective to do it in the company of someone with the empathy and expertise to support and guide you. However, if you are familiar with your psychological history, have experience with your psychological process, and can access the subtle core of your body, you can try this release technique yourself. But before you do either of the two practices in this chapter, please spend some time on the Realization Process practices of inhabiting your body, attuning to fundamental consciousness, and the core breath.

Also, after doing either of the two practices in this chapter, sit for a while, inhabiting your whole body. See how you feel. If you have memories and emotions and if you have no one to speak to, then try writing about them. Spend some time with yourself to understand any new insights that come out of the practices. I recommend that you do these practices no more than twice a week so you have time to integrate and inhabit the areas of your body that were released and that have become more open as a result of the practices.

If you have not yet explored your psychological history and you have had, or think that you may have had, severe trauma in your background, then you should not attempt to do this practice on your own. You can work with a psychotherapist who is also certified in the Realization Process.

PRACTICE Releasing Constrictions from Your Body

Sit upright with your feet on the floor. Close your eyes. Focus on your breathing. Let your breath become calm and even. Now feel that you are inside your feet, inhabiting your feet. Let your breath adjust to you being that far down in your body so that your inhale does not lift you up away from your feet. Now inhabit your whole body. Let yourself feel comfortable, living within your whole body.

Find a place in your body where you feel most comfortable. You can return to inhabiting this part of your body if, at any time, the following release work becomes too intense. As you work with releasing one small area of your body, let yourself observe that work from the vantage point of inhabiting your whole body. You may uncover memories or emotions from your past, but you are still inhabiting your whole body in the present.

Find a place in your body where you feel there is an area of tension.

Find the center of your head, between your ears, the center of the internal space of your head.

From the center of your head, bring your focus within the tension in such a way that the tension moves spontaneously further into the constriction, and it intensifies. As this happens, you may be able to feel the meaning or intention of the movement into constriction (for example, what you are holding back or keeping out).

Are there any memories, images, or emotions as you do this? How old do you feel? What is happening around you? If you formed this constriction in childhood, you may feel the age and the quality of your childhood mentality when you first moved into the constriction. You may even be able to feel and align yourself with this part of yourself that initially moved into the constriction (the agency of the movement).

Now let go of the intensification of the movement into constriction and allow the tension to unfurl along the same pathway. It will only release a little at a time. Repeat this same process several times, opening to any memories, images, or emotions that occur as you do this. You may uncover several different memories, emotions, and ages within the same pattern of binding as you continue to repeat this process.

Inhabit the area that has released. Now inhabit your whole body, including that area.

How the Release Technique Works

In this method, we focus within the rigidity of the holding pattern, in such a way that there is a spontaneous movement within the rigidity toward greater constriction. In other words, we are not moving the pattern further into constriction; we are not exaggerating the constriction. But we are using our focus to penetrate within the tension in a way that evokes a spontaneous movement further into constriction. We focus within the tension, and then we experience the movement. This ensures that the pattern will constrict along the exact pathway that we originally used to produce it, rather than a movement that we impose on it.

Then, when this spontaneous movement further into constriction reaches its zenith, we allow it to let go and unwind along the same pathway. This again means that we are not making a volitional movement into unwinding, but just allowing it to happen and just experiencing it. It will unwind exactly as it was originally constricted.

We are also not breathing into the pattern of constriction, as some body psychotherapy techniques do, but rather focusing within it. This give us access to a more subtle level of the tension than breathing into it provides. There seems to be a subtle level of consciousness, pervading everywhere in the body that is the medium of these movements into constriction. It is not fundamental consciousness itself, but, in a sense, it is right next to FC. This has been referred to in spiritual literature as the causal level of consciousness or *buddhi*. It is buddhi that can open, as it becomes free of constrictions, to gradually realize the "Buddha," your true, unbound nature. In the Realization Process, I call it the "moveable mind." When we focus within the tensions, we can access this subtle "moveable mind" and release the constrictions from their roots.

To be clear, I am speaking about experience, about ways that we can experience ourselves. I am not making a metaphysical claim that there is actually a level of causal consciousness throughout the body. I am saying that we can attune to ourselves in this subtle way that can help us free ourselves of constrictions and inhabit our body fully.

We find the center of the head first, in this technique, so our focus within the constriction is fine and precise enough to access this subtle level of consciousness within the binding. We need to use this precise focus to penetrate within the rigidity so it can move spontaneously further into constriction and then release. Once we can refine our focus without finding the center of our head first, then we no longer need to begin by finding the center of our head.

The Realization Process release technique is not limited to postures, to easily visible organizations of the body, such as cringing or deflating the chest. It can release holding patterns that are deep within the body, that are not even visible, except to a very sensitive observer. So we can, for example, release subtle patterns, such as the shutting down of emotional responsiveness deep within the chest, the barely discernible drawing in of one side of the head so as to limit intelligence in a specific way, or the constriction around our sexual organs that occurred during abuse or during shaming circumstances related to sexual pleasure.

As we repeat the practice of focusing within the constriction and allowing it to move spontaneously into further constriction and release, we can sometimes recognize the original purpose of the constriction. We may remember the event or person that we were protecting ourselves against, for example, or our own responses that we were trying to suppress. Or we may remember our parent's body and realize that the constriction in our body mirrors their pattern of rigidity. This remembrance helps guide us into the precise location and pathway of the constriction.

As the constriction moves along its pathway into release, we often experience the emotions that had been bound in the constriction. If we were holding back anger, that anger may now flare up for expression. If we were suppressing grief, we will find ourselves crying, and our tears may feel like those of a young child. If we were tightening against feeling fear, perhaps so as not to appear vulnerable to a threatening parent or sibling, we may now experience that fear. These emotions are connected with specific memories, and they dissipate as we allow them to move through our body.

We may also be able to feel the age that we were when we formed the pattern. We may experience the fragment of the child's mentality that moved into the constriction. Sometimes we can even align ourselves with this fragment of our childhood mind and with our childhood volition. Even though these constrictions are unconscious and spontaneous reactions to our childhood circumstances, there still seems to be an agent of the movement within the bound constriction. Although we do not make a conscious decision or even notice the movement into the constriction, it is not something that happens to us—it is something we do. When we can align ourselves with that childhood agency, we can open the constriction as easily as opening our hand. People sometimes describe a sense of being trapped within their tensions, as if they are being held or bound against their will. But actually, we are gripping ourselves, and we can let go of that grip.

To release a pattern completely requires repeated practice of the release technique along that same pathway in the body. Repetition makes the rigid, frozen movement of the constriction become increasingly fluid. Also, as we observe this spontaneous movement into constriction, the once-unconscious movement into the pattern becomes conscious. This means that we can become more aware of the tendency to move again into the same constriction when our present-day circumstances are similar to those that first evoked the constriction in our childhood. We can have the choice not to constrict ourselves.

Sometimes people experience these constrictions as areas of darkness or emptiness in their body. But that sense of emptiness or "black hole" is really an area that is particularly tight and dense. It feels like something is missing there because it is missing from your contact with yourself. If you focus within the darkness or emptiness, you may be able to reach the constriction, then allow it to move even further into constriction, and then release.

As we focus on releasing one area of the body, we may feel tensions that we had not been aware of before, in other parts of our body. For example, as we release a tension in our throat, we may feel tension in our diaphragm. This is because we use various parts of our body at the same time in reaction to traumatic circumstances. For example, if expressing anger toward our parent results in severe punishment, we may constrict several parts of our body to keep ourselves from expressing, or even from feeling, our anger. We may hold our breath by constricting our diaphragm at the same time as we close our throat, tense our mouth, and even constrict our eyes to mask our angry expression.

As we release a bound pattern in our body, we may find that the same pattern served different purposes and is also associated with different ages in our childhood. We may use the same pathway of constriction as an infant to diminish the sound of a loudly ticking clock that we use at age eight to block out the sound of our parents fighting. Releasing a pattern from the body may therefore yield various memories, ages, and emotions. Each of these memories can be helpful in revealing the pattern's exact pathway and releasing it completely.

Not all of the tensions in our body are psychologically based. This technique can also help us release patterns of constriction that occurred as a result of a physical injury or a structural imbalance that occurred at birth, for example, through a forceps delivery. There may also be some memory and emotion bound within these physically based constrictions, but even if there is not, we can release them in the same way: by focusing within the tension, allowing it to move further into constriction, and then allowing it to unwind along the same pathway.

Understanding Our Psychological History

People often ask me if it is necessary to understand our past in order to become free of our psychological patterns. Some spiritual practitioners, in particular, believe that since our true nature is deeper than our psychological narrative, that narrative is unimportant and can be ignored. They hope that they can reach their true nature through meditation alone or through positive thinking.

Sometimes we can release a pattern of constriction without learning its purpose in our childhood. Some of our less deeply ingrained patterns can be released just through meditation. And some of our patterns of depression or anger may be, at least, temporarily alleviated by replacing our negative thoughts with happy ones. But our deeply ingrained patterns of constriction will not be released, or stay released, without psychological insight. The labyrinth of constrictions in our body is made of meaning and memory. We cannot access its passageways without understanding its meanings and bringing its memories to present-day awareness.

Conversely, many therapists believe that if we can fully remember a traumatic event, we can avoid or heal the lingering effects of trauma, called post-traumatic stress. We can cease to be haunted by flashbacks of the event or to play out the hypervigilance and hyperreactivity induced by the trauma. But this view does not take into account how we hold the memory of the trauma, and our reaction to it, within the tissues of our body. Memory alone will not free the trauma-based constrictions from our body. Even if we can remember and convey all of the traumatic event in words, our childhood mentality and emotions, bound within the constrictions in our body, will continue to influence our present-day outlook, abilities, and choices.

To free ourselves of these patterns of constriction, we need to both focus within the bound tissues of the body and to understand the initial purpose or purposes of the binding. If we do not understand the situations that led to our patterns of constriction, we are much more likely to reorganize them or to augment their rigidity whenever similar situations arise in our lives. We need to know, for example, that we constricted our capacity to love in response to a parent that was not capable of feeling love or else we will continue to constrict ourselves whenever anyone is unloving toward us. But if we understand the exact events and relationships that produced our patterns of constriction, we will be able to release this binding and retain this release no matter what circumstances we encounter. We will be able to remain open in our present-day lives and relationships.

To know our psychological history can also help us to feel at peace with ourselves. We may feel compassion and respect for ourselves when we can actually uncover, within our body, the memories of the situations that challenged us as children and the ways in which we managed to protect and preserve ourselves.

An Illustration of the Release Technique

Christine came to work with me several years ago. On the phone, she said that she wanted to do the release work. Her voice was strong and clear, and yet at the same time, somewhat childlike, and apologetic. When we met for the first time, I was impressed by her vitality. She was in her early forties, and dressed exotically, in velvet pants and a colorfully patterned silk top. I felt happy sitting with her and somehow reassured by the strength of her presence. At first glance, she seemed delighted with life, and I wondered where she felt herself to be constricted. But when she began to speak, to introduce herself to me, I heard again that childlike lilt in her voice. Watching carefully, I noticed that, although she gave the impression of being grounded and secure, there was an upward lift in her throat, upper chest, and solar plexus area.

Christine had already been practicing the attunement to fundamental consciousness and the core breath with one of the certified Realization Process teachers, so I was able to proceed directly into the release work with her.

I asked her to tell me something about her childhood and if there had been any severe trauma. "Not severe, no. I wouldn't say that," she responded with an engaging smile. "But my father was often furious, and my mother was always anxious." As she said that, the upward lift in her body became more pronounced, and for a moment, she looked like a frightened child.

"Were you afraid of your father?" I asked.

"He was pretty scary when he really got going. I wouldn't say he was always furious; it was more unpredictable." Now she put a hand protectively to her upper chest.

"Where in your body do you feel tension?"

"My throat. And my upper chest," she said.

I began by guiding her through the release technique in her throat.

"Find the tension in your throat. And see if you can bring your focus deep within the tension, in such a way that it becomes even more constricted."

I watched Christine make contact with the internal space of her throat and then focus more deeply into what seemed like a knot around her larynx. As she did that, the knot seemed to tighten further.

"And now let go a little." I usually use the words "a little" so people do not attempt to let go of the whole constriction at once. What we let go of is the intensification of the constriction that occurred when we focused within the tension. Then there is spontaneous (nonvolitional) unwinding along the pathway of the constriction.

"What do you feel when you do that?"

"I felt a little trickle of energy inside my throat."

"That's good. Now do exactly the same thing again."

We repeated the same sequence of focusing within the tension, allowing it to move further into constriction and then letting it go. By the third repetition, the constriction moved further into release, and Christine could feel more energy moving through her throat.

Suddenly, her eyes filled with tears, and she again put her hand to her upper chest.

"When my father yelled at me, it was like he suddenly didn't love me anymore. That was the scariest part of it, the saddest part."

Her tears released some of the tension in her upper chest, although I knew that in future sessions, we would return to do further release work in that part of her body.

"Now, inhabit your whole throat area," I said. "And attune to the quality of your voice, your potential to speak, within your neck."

As she did this, the "new territory" that she had gained from releasing the constriction gave her more access to her throat and more sense of internal space within her throat. She also felt more connection between her throat and her chest. When she spoke, we both noticed that her vocal tone had become fuller and more resonant. She no longer had that childlike, apologetic sound to her voice.

PRACTICE Finding and Releasing Constrictions in Relation to a Parent

This is a practice that I teach to help people find some of the ways in which they organized and constricted themselves in relation to a parent. In order to do this practice, first practice inhabiting your body and attuning to fundamental consciousness. Again, if you have had severe trauma with one of your parents, then it is important to do this practice with the support of a psychotherapist who is certified in the Realization Process.

Sit upright with your feet on the floor. Close your eyes. Focus on your breathing. Let your breath become calm and even. Now feel that you are inside your feet, inhabiting your feet. Let your breath adjust to you being that far down in your body so your inhale does not lift you up away from your feet.

Now inhabit your whole body. Let yourself feel comfortable, living within your whole body. Find the space outside of your body. Experience that the space inside and outside of your body is the same, continuous space.

Picture your mother or father in front of you.

Experience that the space that pervades you also pervades your parent.

Bring your attention to the space pervading your whole body and your parent's head. (Remain within your body as you do this. Do not project yourself into your parent's head.) Notice any changes anywhere in your own body as you do this.

Bring your attention to the space pervading your whole body and your parent's neck. Notice any changes anywhere in your own body as you do this.

Bring your attention to the space pervading your whole body and your parent's chest. Notice any changes anywhere in your own body as you do this.

Bring your attention to the space pervading your whole body and your parent's midsection. Notice any changes anywhere in your own body as you do this.

Bring your attention to the space pervading your whole body and your parent's pelvis. Notice any changes anywhere in your own body as you do this.

If any area of your body constricted during this exercise, go back to that part of your own body. If several areas in your body constricted, choose one. Focus within the constriction so it moves further into constriction. Let yourself feel why you are constricting yourself in relation to your parent. How old do you feel? Do you feel any emotion as you do this? Do you have any memories? Are you mirroring your parent's constriction or reacting to your parent?

When you can feel the constriction intensify, let go of it and let it move toward release.

Repeat this again: focus within the constriction; let it move toward the constricted position. Let go of it and let it move toward release.

Now, continuing to picture your parent in front of you, see if you can inhabit the part of your body that you had constricted. Attune to the quality of your being associated with that part of your body (for example, understanding, voice, love, power, gender).

Dissolve the image of your parent. Feel that you are inside your whole body and make deep internal contact with yourself.

The Importance of Patience and Kindness

The anecdotes throughout this book can make it seem like release and healing happens very quickly, and sometimes it does. But in general, becoming free of our constrictions is a slow, gradual process. It requires revisiting our main holding patterns many times, as well as often finding new ones as we go more deeply within our body and our history. To be completely free of psychological constrictions is an ideal that we approach but may never completely reach. However, we do not need to release all of our constrictions in order to be able to inhabit our body and know ourselves as the pervasive space of fundamental consciousness. And the more we are able to realize ourselves as FC, the easier it becomes to release our binding. Also, even the slightest release can make a big difference in the way we feel and in our access to the essential qualities and capacities of our being.

It can sometimes be tiring to release these constrictions. It is just as if you have been holding your hand in a fist for twenty years or fifty years, and then you open your hand. Your hand would feel achy and tired. So get plenty of rest after doing any release work. Although this does not happen often, people sometimes feel a little trembling in the area that they released. They may feel a little light-headed, or even, if the memories they released were very toxic, they may feel nauseous. These symptoms will pass in a day or two, and then you will probably feel energized.

Please be patient with your healing process. The slowness of the process gives you time to integrate the newly freed parts of yourself. So please be very patient and very kind to yourself.

It is most important to conclude each release session with inhabiting the part of the body that you have been releasing. This allows the newly released part of yourself to become part of the internal, unified ground of your being, part of your wholeness. The possessing of the newly released space within your body enables the release to be a lasting change in the way you inhabit your body.

9

TOWARD HEALING ANXIETY AND DEPRESSION

The inherent nature of the Self is bliss.

RAMANA MAHARSHI

O ur memories of trauma, and the chronically bound emotions in our body that are associated with them, can produce chronic patterns of anxiety and depression. In this chapter, I look at how the Realization Process can help alleviate these patterns. I do not intend these practices to heal severe depression, anxiety, or bipolar disorder. For the sake of safety, these more severe forms of emotional pain need to be treated chemically. And any chronic state of anxiety or depression should be approached through insight and verbal process, with the help of a trained, compassionate therapist. However, the Realization Process practices can be an effective supplement to both medical and psychotherapeutic treatments.

Releasing the Pattern of Anxiety

Existential philosophers claim that anxiety is unavoidable. They say that our knowledge that we are mortal, along with the energy and will that we employ to ignore that knowledge, makes anxiety a quintessentially human condition. The more questioning or rejecting we are of unprovable notions, such as heaven and reincarnation, the more anxious we may be.

Buddhist philosophy claims that our anxiety stems from the illusion of our separateness and the feelings of isolation, vulnerability, and defensiveness that emerge from that illusion. In the Realization Process, this illusion of separateness is understood to be a constructed protective barrier between ourselves and our environment that has become bound in the tissues of our body. The trauma-based constrictions in our body cut us off from contact with both ourselves and others. This constructed, defended separateness can produce anxiety, engendering fear and suspicion of other people, and the need to continually shore up our defenses against them.

Anxiety is also a direct result of trauma. If our childhood environment is particularly abusive or unpredictable, we may become chronically anxious and vigilant to our surroundings. Any memory of having been overpowered or in any way abused may produce an ongoing fear of the recurrence of that trauma.

Over time, anxiety may become a chronically held emotional state within our body and hypervigilance may become a rigidly held pattern within our senses. Our focus may become chronically imbalanced to the world outside of ourselves, rather than to the internal space of our own body. We all live to some extent on the surface of ourselves, but in a hypervigilant state, our focus extends in a static, ongoing way out into the environment.

The movement of anxiety within the body is upward. We have the saying, "My heart was in my throat." When we are anxious, we feel that the internal space of our chest lifts upward. We tend to experience our breath only in our upper chest and to breathe in short gasps. If we are anxious for much of our childhood, this upward lift and constricted breath becomes a chronic pattern.

Just as with all of our holding patterns, we may also mirror our parents' held pattern of anxiety. As an emotional condition, anxiety can permeate our environment. If our parents were often anxious, then the air we breathe as children and the atmosphere that we absorb within our body may be permeated with anxiety. This emotion may become held within our body and in our memory of our surroundings. As adults, we carry this internal feeling and external atmosphere of anxiety with us wherever we go, even when our present circumstances do not call for anxiety at all.

People who are anxious often feel "thin-skinned." Life seems to impinge directly on them, without the buffer that other people seem to have. They feel bombarded and even shattered by abrasive sounds, sights, and smells and by the emotional and physical presences of other people. As the poet Yeats described, it feels like the "center does not hold."

Inhabiting the body and accessing the subtle vertical core of the body can give us more sense of distance from the sensory and emotional stimuli in our environment. As we inhabit our body and attune to the pervasive space of fundamental consciousness, we can begin to let go of chronic patterns of hypervigilance. If we can experience FC as a perceptual field, as a sensory receptivity, then we can use our senses with much less effort. We no longer feel drawn out of our body toward the objects of our perception.

As we know ourselves as fundamental consciousness, we find that the center does hold—we have a palpable sense that the basic unity of our being cannot be disturbed. It is "self-existent" and "self-coherent." Experience passes through us without altering this basic, cohesive sense of our own existence. The practice of Perception as Fundamental Consciousness in chapter 6 can help you to let go of the pattern of hypervigilance and allow your experience to occur in the pervasive space of your being without altering your fundamental experience of unity.

The practice of inhabiting the body can be used specifically to counter the upward displacement in the body that is often caused by anxiety. As you inhabit each part of your body, give yourself a moment to settle downward within the area. But do not press downward and do not collapse the outside of your body. This is a gentle, internal settling within each part of the body. It is usually particularly important, as an antidote for anxiety, to settle within the chest and neck. The instruction for this is:

Inhabit the internal space of your chest. Settle within your chest. Feel that you are "sitting in your heart." Inhabit your neck. Settle within your neck.

Inhabiting the lower part of your body, your feet, legs, and pelvis, can also help you feel more grounded so you let go of the upward holding pattern in your body. You can feel this sitting, standing, and walking. The instruction for this is:

Inhabit your feet. Let your breath adjust to you being that far down in your body so your inhale does not lift you up away from your feet.

Let yourself feel that there is no separation between your feet and ground.

Walk across the room. With each step, feel again that you have "no separation" with ground.

The practice of Foundational Grounding in chapter 3 can help you settle within your whole body.

As you explore your childhood history, you may be able to find the origin of your anxiety. Then you can focus the Realization Process practices with more precision to heal your anxiety. In the following anecdote, for example, a woman specifically counters a chronic sense of imminent danger by using the embodiment practice to cultivate an internal sense of safety.

When Margaret came to work with me, she said that she felt a constant low-level anxiety, but she did not know what caused it. She felt very happy in her present life but could not rid herself of the sense that something terrible was about to happen. As I began to lead her through inhabiting her body, her anxiety increased.

"It feels dangerous to be in here, to be in my body," she said.

"What is the danger?" I asked.

When she attuned directly to the feeling of anxiety in her body, she felt as if she were a very young child, around two years old. Then she suddenly had a vivid memory of her father's angry face, and his chest "swelled up like a cobra."

"It was so long ago," she said. "My mother and I left him when I was three years old. I haven't thought about him in a long time. But now I can see his face. He was always enraged. My mother was terrified of him. He would strike out at her without warning, and once he hit me across my legs. That's when my mother finally got up the courage to leave him."

Although it had been many years since she had lived with her father, she was still carrying in her body the memory of being in imminent danger from his anger. As I continued to guide her through the practice of inhabiting her body, I asked her to take a moment, in each part of her body, to experience a sense of safety. The instruction was, "Feel that you are in your feet. Let yourself feel safe within your feet," repeated in each part of her body. Gradually, she was able to counter the long-held pattern of anxiety in her body by cultivating an internal sense of safety.

You can also use the embodiment practice to cultivate a feeling of calm, peacefulness, courage, or any quality that you feel you need, in each part of your body. Use whatever quality seems most appropriate as an antidote for the particular source of your anxiety.

Another way to heal anxiety is by clearing the space outside of your body. Our memory of our childhood environment not only affects the space within our body; we also hold that memory in the space around our body. If there was a sense of threat in the atmosphere, for example, we need to bring our present-day consciousness to that memory in order to release it.

Greta told me that she had no reason to be anxious; it was just her nature. But I do not believe that anxiety is anyone's basic nature. As we spoke about her childhood, it became clear that both her parents had been extremely anxious. They transmitted this anxiety to her in their extreme caution and concern for her safety and in the way in which they regarded and spoke of the "outside world." They also filled the atmosphere in their home with the feeling of their anxiety.

"It seems like the air I breathed was anxious," Greta said.

I asked Greta to see if she could feel her childhood atmosphere around her body. She was surprised to be able to find this remembered atmosphere around her easily. It had always been there without her noticing it, continuing to influence her mood.

"The air around me feels like it is full of anxiety," she said. "No wonder it feels like the air I breathed. It really was."

I asked her to try to attune to the present-day atmosphere around her—the atmosphere in my office.

"That feels completely different," she said. As she switched back and forth a few times between her childhood atmosphere and the present atmosphere, the anxiety around her began to dissipate. I suggested that she practice the same attunement in her own home, remembering her childhood atmosphere and then feeling the atmosphere that surrounds her now.

Greta had also kept herself in an anxious state by continuing to hold anxiety in her breath. She found, again to her surprise, that she could attune to the anxiety within her breath. "It feels like some sort of metallic thread inside my breath," she said. When she could feel this clearly, she was able to expunge the anxiety from her breath and to breathe the air in her present environment. Gradually, the feeling of anxiety both within and around her body dissolved. She was able to let go of the habit of anxiety that she had carried from her childhood into adulthood and enjoy the peacefulness of her present life.

Releasing the Pattern of Depression

Just like anxiety, depression can be a habitual organization of ourselves. When we are depressed, we may come up with various rationales for our mood, but the roots of chronic depression are usually in our childhood or in reaction to losses or failures that we suffered later in life. If we can find the actual origin of our depression, we can address it more effectively. Depression is often the result of long-suppressed sadness or anger. Locating the original cause of these emotions often allows the depression to be experienced in its original form of anger or grief, and then to flow through us and dissipate.

Just as we may mirror our parents' anxiety or absorb the atmosphere of anxiety in our childhood home, we may mirror our parent's depression and absorb within our body the general atmosphere of depression in which we grew up. We may carry with us into adulthood the black cloud that surrounded us in our childhood home, even when the present circumstances of our lives are not at all depressing.

Sarah came to work with me because she felt an emptiness in her life that she could not seem to overcome. She lived with a man she loved in a house that she loved, and her work made her feel useful as well as financially secure. Yet she woke each day with a feeling of darkness and heaviness in her body, and a sense of dread. Once she was up and active, she was no longer aware of this feeling, but it would surface again if she sat and relaxed. When I asked her to find the sense of darkness and dread in her body, she was shocked to discover a deep well of despair within her whole body. "I feel like I want to die," she said. I asked her if there had been any early losses in her life, but she could not think of any.

I asked her how old she felt when she attuned to this darkness in her body. At first this question made no sense to her because the feeling was always there in her present life. But after a few minutes, she suddenly said, "I feel like I'm around six years old." "What was happening in your life when you were six?" I asked. It took Sarah a little while to remember but finally she said, "That must have been when my grandmother moved in with us."

Her grandmother had been a holocaust survivor and moved in with Sarah's family when her husband died. "She just sat by the window, completely still," Sarah remembered, "and stared out into the street. The whole atmosphere in the house changed after that. I don't remember any laughter. It was like we all had to be so careful around her. Like she was some dark spirit that made everything go still around her." Suddenly Sarah had an insight into the dread that she feels when she wakes up in the morning. "In the morning, before I went to school, she would be sitting at the kitchen table, and I would have to have breakfast with her. She seemed to look right through me."

"What do you feel when you picture her there?" I asked.

"I feel angry," Sarah said. Then she covered her mouth with her hand. "That's terrible, isn't it? I feel so angry at her. She suffered so much. But it was like she destroyed all our joy." She looked at me guiltily. I encouraged her to feel the anger that she had never been allowed to express or even to feel before. "I wasn't allowed to laugh out loud. If I ran in the house or made any kind of noise, my parents would make me stop right away. I never even had friends over because she would be sitting there, like a ghost, sucking the happiness out of the room."

Having allowed her anger to move through her, Sarah sat for a moment silently. Then she said, "And I also feel pity. God, she was so sad. I've never seen anyone so sad." She began to cry, very deeply, tears that had, like her anger, never been allowed to flow. "We never talked about what she had gone through," Sarah sobbed. "We just tiptoed around her. But I can feel her sadness in my whole body."

After this, Sarah felt relieved of some of the depression, but there was still some work to do before she could let go of it completely. She said that she could feel her grandmother's grief even inside of her bones. For several months, in her meditation, she practiced inhabiting her bones and exhaling the sadness out of them. With this practice, she was finally able to release the pattern of depression from her body.

Ongoing loneliness can also result in depression. This feeling may be exacerbated by childhood memories. Old losses that have not been thoroughly grieved and accepted may give rise to a chronic sense of having been abandoned or unloved. Uncovering the original losses and allowing ourselves to experience our bereavement and to mourn can help alleviate this type of depression.

Patrick was deeply depressed when I first met him. He said that he felt betrayed and abandoned by everyone he had ever loved. Now he had cut off ties with everyone in his life and was living in almost complete isolation. "I don't need anyone," he said. As we did the Realization Process practices, he was able to feel layers of bitterness and grief, and finally deep longing within his chest. This feeling of longing, that he had never let himself feel before, was helpful to him. It began to motivate him to come out of his isolation. But as he made contact with himself in his body, he also began to feel more tolerance for being alone, less bitter, and less lonely in his solitude. He said that as he inhabited each part of his body, he felt like he was "meeting the beloved."

Depression is often maintained through inner monologue about our personal shortcomings or the futility of effort or ambition or the general bleakness of life. This self-talk may be unconscious, or it may become so much our ordinary state that we do not notice it. It often takes the shape of self-loathing. This self-critical voice may run in the background of our conscious awareness as a negative commentary on all of our actions and character. It is a constant negative feedback loop, keeping us from accomplishing anything of merit so that we seem ever more deserving of failure and self-derision. It can keep us from seeing anything positive in the world so that our view of life becomes increasingly dark. The antidote for negative self-talk is to bring it into awareness so we can question and test the validity of our negative beliefs. We may also find that our self-criticism is the internalization of criticism that we received as a child or adolescent and that it does not reflect our own true assessment of ourselves.

The Realization Process practices can also help counter feelings of self-loathing. As I described in a previous chapter, when we experience the inherent qualities of our being, such as the love within our chest and the intelligence within our brain, we know that we cannot be that hateful deficient person that we had thought. We cannot hate a person who seems to be made of love.

Attuning to fundamental consciousness can also help alleviate depression because it is experienced as luminous. The experience of light has often been associated with spiritual experience. In the Gospel of St. Matthew, Christ says, "If thy eye is single, thy whole body will be full of light." Although there are different translations and interpretations of this "single eye," the internal illumination of the body seems to hold across different versions of the text.

When we attune to fundamental consciousness pervading our environment, the world becomes more radiant. Everything that we perceive is suffused with a very subtle luminosity. When we experience FC pervading our body, one of the ways we experience this is that we are made of light. We have an internal "feel" of light, and we can also perceive this internal radiance in other people. This inner and outer luminosity can very effectively dispel the sense of darkness and heaviness in the body that accompanies depression.

We can facilitate this transformation from darkness into light by specifically cultivating this aspect of our embodiment. The instruction for this is: Feel that you inhabit your feet. Feel that you are made of light within your feet. Feel that you are in your ankles and lower legs. Feel that you are made of light within your ankles and lower legs.

You may notice that I am not saying "Feel that your feet are made of light," but rather "Feel you are made of light within your feet." I do not want people to imagine that their body is something separate from themselves. We do not have a luminous body. We are the luminosity of fundamental consciousness, within our body.

We can also practice the core breath in a way that helps cultivate our experience of luminosity. We can experience or visualize the core points—the center of the head, chest, and pelvis—as made of light. As we initiate the breath within each core point, the light kindles; it very slightly intensifies.

People who are depressed will sometimes find the heart center a little too low. We have the expression "heavy heart." When someone is depressed, it may look and feel as though they are carrying a heavy burden within their chest. When you find your heart center, make sure that you can access the whole internal space of your body, just by being in your heart center. This will help prevent you from finding the point either too high, as we may do when we are anxious, or too low, as we may do when we are chronically depressed.

Practicing the core breath within the heart center can also help alleviate depression. As we refine our breath within the heart center, we can more easily access a subtle emotional quality within our chest that seems to be behind, and beneath, the burden of depression. This can help us recognize that the darkness and heaviness that we have carried in our body is not our actual nature. There is light, and an actual feeling of happiness, within the darkness.

Just as fundamental consciousness can be experienced as luminosity, it can also be experienced as bliss. I sometimes ask people to attune to the emotional aspect of FC as bliss. This is not a peak experience, but an ongoing experience of contentment and well-being that can remain stable even when circumstances are difficult. Once we know ourselves as FC, we can always find this happiness within our chest, and even within our whole body and environment.

The reason that I do not always include the instruction to attune to the emotional aspect of fundamental consciousness as bliss is that I do not want people to attempt to manufacture bliss. This is an attunement to ourselves, a way that we can experience ourselves, rather than an imitation of a feeling.

Earlier in this book, I included a practice for attuning to awareness, emotion, and physical sensation as the three main qualities of fundamental consciousness. That practice is important for opening our whole body and being to FC. However, there are other ways that we can also experience this ground of being. The following is a practice to attune to fundamental consciousness as emptiness, luminosity, and bliss. This practice can be particularly helpful in alleviating anxiety and depression.

PRACTICE Three Attunements to Fundamental Consciousness

Sit with your back straight and your eyes open.

Feel that you inhabit your whole body. Find the space outside of your body. Feel that the space inside and outside of your body is the same continuous space; it pervades you.

Let yourself experience that the space that pervades you also pervades your whole environment.

Attune to the pervasive space as emptiness, as sheer transparency.

Attune to the pervasive space as luminosity.

Attune to the pervasive space as bliss.

Attune to bliss and emptiness at the same time. Bring in the quality of luminosity as well and let the three qualities blend together. Sit for a few minutes as the pervasive space of emptiness, bliss, and luminosity.

10

TRAUMA AND SPIRITUAL TEACHINGS

Every being is changed to a perfectly
coherent radiance made transparent through
the illumination of the transcendent.

YUASA YASUO

Many of the same people who are motivated to heal from the wounds of trauma are also drawn to the spiritual paths that are readily available today. The Realization Process, in particular, because it is also a path of nondual, spiritual awakening, attracts many people who have also spent years meditating or engaging in other spiritual practices. In the Realization Process, we open into the fundamental, unified ground of our being as we heal the bodily constrictions and negative beliefs that are based on our history of trauma. In this way, psychological healing and spiritual awakening become the same process toward maturity. The experience of ourselves and our world as suffused with the same subtle radiant consciousness is the natural condition of that maturity.

Any spiritual technique that facilitates our inward contact with ourselves, that guides us to open our heart and mind, can help us in this process of becoming whole, mature human beings. However, some spiritual teachings or misinterpretations of those teachings, can also exacerbate rather than heal our psychological pain. Some of the most popular spiritual teachings in the West today teach people that they do not exist as human beings, that emotional responsiveness should be overcome for spiritual maturity, that thinking gets in the way of enlightenment, and that our individual agency is an illusion. In this chapter, I look at some of the ways in which these teachings can obstruct both psychological healing and spiritual awakening.

Abusive Teachers

As I described in my last book, *Belonging Here*, the sensitivity that is both required and cultivated by most spiritual teachings brings with it its own specific psychological challenges. Spiritually sensitive people can be deeply wounded, especially as children, even by small, ordinary lapses in love by one's parents. They can grow up feeling out of sync with their family members and peers, attuned to subtle sensory experiences that are not discernible to other people. They may feel bombarded and overwhelmed by their environment and find it traumatic to live in the imperfect, suffering world.

Our history of trauma can make us susceptible to spiritual teachers who abuse their power and position. We may feel a desperate need for a mother or father figure who can finally really know us or for someone who can provide us with safe shelter from the chaotic world. The depth of our pain may make us easy prey for teachers offering bliss and transcendence and cause us to be willing to purchase that bliss at any price. Determined to be free from the hypocrisy and the social masks we see around us, we may surrender our better judgement to accept "whole cloth" the claims of a person who seems to possess otherworldly knowledge. Desperate to be accepted and loved, we may easily be fooled by the sexual manipulations of someone who appears to single us out for attention.

Sometimes when we find a teacher or a spiritual path, we feel that here is someone or something that is finally worthy of our pure devotion. Although the love that we have felt for our parents and siblings and the love that we originally may have felt for ourselves has become distorted and damaged by the traumatic events of our childhood, here is finally a place where we can give free rein to our love, a place where we can feel and express our goodness. If this devotion is met with integrity by the teacher at the helm, then the path we have chosen really is a place in which we can feel a childlike devotion to someone more mature than ourselves, and over time, have that devotion transform into mature love—love that does not require us to make sacrifices of essential parts of our own humanness, such as our ability for independent, original thought, or our love for other people outside of the spiritual path. But if our devotion is not met with integrity, it may not contribute to our own growth but contribute only to the glory of the teacher. It is most important, whatever path or teacher we choose, that we understand that the path is for our own awakening, not for the benefit of the teacher or the spiritual school.

The Question of Personal Identity

The main conflict between methods of psychological healing and some interpretations of Asian spiritual teachings is regarding the issue of personal identity. Within both Buddhism and Hinduism, there are teachings that claim either that the phenomenal world is basically nonexistent or that our individual sense of existence is an illusion, or both. Once, years ago, I attended a talk by Jean Klein, a revered teacher in the Hindu nondual (Advaita) tradition. After the talk, a psychotherapist stood up in the audience and asked how he could convey this profound teaching to his clients. Jean Klein said, "Most important is that you do not tell him that he is a person. If you imply that he is a person, then you contribute to his suffering."

There are many different philosophies within Asian religions. One of the main debates between them is whether there is a ground of existence that can be realized as the ground of our own being or whether there is no ground, nothing beyond the changing flux of experience. In the Realization Process, we uncover the experience of a ground of being, pervading our body and environment at the same time. In this way, we achieve deepened internal contact with our individual being, and at the same time, we experience oneness with our environment. This means that we mature as individuals as we transcend our individuality.

The idea that we are both separate and unified with others is at odds with those teachings that ask people to eradicate their sense of existing as individuals. Once at a Realization Process workshop, a young man challenged me. "If you feel pain in your knee," he demanded, "do you say that it is your pain, or do you say that it is just pain?" "I say that it is my pain," I answered. "No!" he insisted, shocked and disappointed that I would get this wrong. "There is no 'you.' There is just pain." But when we know ourselves as fundamental consciousness, subjectivity and the content of subjectivity are unified. There is no known without a knower. Knower and known are one and occur simultaneously.

For each of us, the pervasive ground of fundamental consciousness is experienced as the deepest, most authentic contact that we can have with our individual being. As we constrict ourselves in response to trauma, we fragment ourselves. For example, the constrictions in our throat may cut off our ability to think from our ability to feel. We cease to be able to function as whole individuals. In severe trauma, people may experience that they leave their body and watch the traumatic event from above. Even when the traumatic event is over, this sense of disembodiment may stay with them for the rest of their lives. The teaching of no-self, or non-existence, can exacerbate this dissociation, rather than heal it. It can cause the dedicated spiritual seeker to further fragment and diminish themselves, to disown their own thoughts, feelings, and sensations.

I have met several people who refuse to use the word "I," referring instead to themselves as "this one," or as in "the one known as Bob has been feeling depressed lately." This interpretation, or misinterpretation, of the Buddhist teaching of selflessness, splits the subject from the object of experience. It splits "Bob" from whomever is referring to Bob. It exacerbates the fragmentation and self-loathing that are already prevalent aspects of human experience in general and the most common results of trauma in particular. If all we are is the passing flux of sensory stimuli, then who we are is an object, something we only witness: "this one." But who is watching this changing array?

We can tell when someone is not quite connected, not quite authentic, for example when someone is not really smiling. But connected to what? The ninth-century Zen master, Rinzai, says in a lecture to his students, "Who then can understand the Dharma and can listen to it? The one here before your very eyes, brilliantly clear and shining without any form—there he is who can understand the Dharma you are listening to. Ceaselessly he is right here, conspicuously present."[1]

For me, the fact that we do exist, that there really is someone here who listens and speaks and sees and hears, is far more mysterious and compelling and more accurate, than the idea that we do not exist.

Beyond the persuasiveness of their teacher's authority, there are often deeper, more hidden motivations for self-eradication that are related to a person's history of trauma. One woman told me, "Nothing can hurt me, because there is no 'me' here to experience the pain." If we pretend that we do not exist, then we will not feel uncomfortable because there will be no one there to feel it. If we still feel uncomfortable, after decades of attempting to not exist, it is because a small part of us still feels that we do exist. We must then try harder to abolish even the tiniest sense of existing. In this interpretation, Buddhism has become a punishment for being human, rather than a way to overcome suffering. Some people embrace this punishment because of their self-loathing or because they are promised some sort of perfection if they can endure it.

This is not just a destructive interpretation of Buddhist teachings; it is misleading. Buddhism is primarily concerned with finding and removing the cause of suffering. It is a method of achieving happiness. Even the teaching of no-self is meant, as I understand it, not as a metaphysical assertion but as way to let go of our manipulation of life. It is taught as a way to help people clear out habitual modes of perception and mental elaboration so we can experience directly the ever-changing radiant display of life.

Rinzai describes the "who" that we are as formless and brilliantly shining. He said, "Followers of the way: The Dharma of the heart has no form and pervades the ten directions. In the eye, it is called seeing; in the ear, hearing; in the nose, smelling; in the mouth, talking; in the hands, grasping; in the feet, walking. Fundamentally, it is one light; differentiated, it becomes the six senses."[2]

This is where the Asian teachings and the goals of psychotherapy converge. We are trying to get through to that one light that is who we really are. The one who is hearing, speaking, knowing, feeling. Not some idea of ourselves. Not a constrained, diminished or constructed version of ourselves. And not an object, but a subject. This is who we all, to some extent, lose touch with very early in our lives.

The Question of Free Will

The spontaneity that we gain when we realize fundamental consciousness has caused some spiritual teachers to speculate that we might be impelled by some force beyond ourselves, that we do not really have agency or free will of our own. But I do not think that this is an accurate or necessary conclusion to make from the fluid responsiveness that is an aspect of nondual realization. For at the same time that we let go of our grip on ourselves, we also become conscious and present everywhere within ourselves. This gives us control over our responses everywhere in our body and being. As fundamental consciousness, we always have a choice: we can surrender to the dance of responsiveness or control the movements of our responses at any time.

As I described earlier in this book, any trauma that has involved someone overpowering us can rob us of our sense of agency, our ability to make choices, and our ability to recognize and pursue our ambitions. For this reason, a spiritual teaching that claims that we are all the pawns of some force beyond ourselves, or that we are just cogs in a larger system, can contribute to our traumatic wounding.

Thinking and Feeling

Along with the attempt not to exist, some popular spiritual teachers today are also guiding their students to not feel or think. The main, traditional practice in the Hindu nondual (Advaita) teachings is called "not this, not this" (Sanskrit: *neti neti*). It is a cognitive practice in which the practitioner says to him or herself: "I am not my body. I am not my feelings. I am not my thoughts." The purpose of the practice is to recognize what is left when we dis-identify from the content of our experience. What is left is the primary ground of being, the true "I" who experiences body, feelings, and thoughts. But this teaching has been interpreted by some teachers to mean that we should not have any content of experience. That the truly enlightened person does not think or feel or sense.

However, when we know ourselves as fundamental consciousness, all of the content of our experience moves more deeply and fluidly through us. We feel more deeply and think more clearly, more creatively, as we allow life to flow. Although our fundamental identity is not our thoughts or feelings, we still have thoughts and feelings.

As we let go of our protective constrictions, the childhood memories of trauma lose their emotional charge and so have less effect on our present life. This means that when we have an emotional response, we do not have that extra "wallop" of stored up anger, grief, or fear. As we heal and mature, our emotions become more relevant, both in their triggers and intensity, to our present situations. But they are still an important enriching and guiding aspect of our lives. We are still emotionally responsive to the world around us.

And we do still think. Although it might be helpful at the beginning of one's practice to observe one's thoughts and attempt to curb them, once we experience ourselves as fundamental consciousness, then our thoughts also move fluidly. Our habitual tape loops and obsessive thoughts abate, and we can receive fresh insights and ideas. Even "mental elaboration," our thoughts about the objects of our perception, does not interfere with our clear, direct perception of our surroundings.

There has also been some misunderstanding about the popular spiritual concept of being "in the moment." Being present in the moment does not mean that we are somehow fixated on an external, sensory experience. The present moment includes both our internal and external experience. This internal experience, in the present moment, can include memories of the past, preferences for this or that, and plans or anticipation of future events. Our thoughts move through the stable ground of fundamental consciousness, and that ground is always in the present moment, no matter what content is flowing through it. Spiritual awakening does not make us into zombies. All of our faculties for perception, sensation, emotion, and any type of cognition become more fully functional when we know ourselves as that primary "who" that lives in the ground of our being.

Conclusion

Although it can be helpful to concentrate our heart and mind in devotion to another person or lineage, or to empty ourselves of old habits and ideas by surrendering to something that seems greater than ourselves, all of these spiritual practices are in the service of freeing the spiritual nature that is already present within us. When we can let go of our grasp on ourselves, through any method of healing or spiritual practice, we become more of who we are, not less. We become more capable of love and understanding and self-expression and strength and pleasure. Wholeness is our actual shape, hidden within our constricted shape, oneness is our actual relationship with our world and happiness arises spontaneously as an inherent aspect of our being. If we want to experience happiness, even bliss, and to know and live as our essential goodness, we only need to make inward contact with ourselves, to live within our own body.

PRACTICE   **Oneness in Nature**

Stand outside, on the earth, with your eyes open.

Feel that you are inside your feet. Feel that there is no separation between you and the ground.

Feel that you are inside your whole body. Find the space outside your body. Experience that the space inside and outside your body is the same continuous space.

Bring your focus down to the earth. Experience that the space that pervades you also pervades the earth.

Bring your focus up to the sky. Experience that the space that pervades you also pervades the sky.

Bring your focus to a tree. Experience that the space that pervades you also pervades the tree. Let yourself experience the life within the tree as well as the space pervading it.

Walk, remaining inside your body, and attuned to the space pervading you and the nature around you.

EPILOGUE

An ancient Hindu prayer asks to be led from ignorance to truth. Our spiritual reality is the same as the essential truth of our personhood. As we dissolve our protective shell and realize our oneness with other life, we realize ourselves. Within our own body, we find the unified, responsive, spontaneous being that we have always known somewhere in the background of all our experience. This landing in truth, this tangible feeling of reality, when we have been living in limitation and disguise, is one of the most fulfilling experiences available to human beings.

ACKNOWLEDGMENTS

My gratitude to everyone who has come to work with me over the last four decades— your questions have helped me clarify this work, your practice has helped me trust its validity, and your presence in my life has brought so much pleasure and light to my own spiritual path. I especially thank my readers for your valuable suggestions: Zoran Josipovic, Roma Hammel, Candace Cave, Robert Kenny, Sally Schwager, Marcia Haarer, Catherine Lilly, Jon Hansen, Laurie Dawson, and Liz Hartshorn.

APPENDIX

FOR THERAPISTS AND OTHER HEALERS WORKING WITH THE REALIZATION PROCESS

Part I: The Therapeutic Relationship

When, as therapists, we can experience fundamental consciousness pervading ourselves and our clients, the therapeutic relationship is transformed in several ways. Our own presence is more centered, grounded, and empathic; we can track our internal responses to our clients more clearly; our perception of our clients is more refined; and we are more open to the spontaneous emergence of the healing process.

The Therapist's Presence

It is widely accepted, in the current field of psychotherapy, that one of the most healing components of the psychotherapeutic process is the relationship between the client and the therapist. One of the biggest shifts that has occurred over the history of psychotherapy is in the client-therapist relationship, especially regarding how personally connected we should be when we sit with a client.

Freud recommended that the analyst's awareness be a "hovering attention" that does not interfere with or interact in any way with

185

the patient's narrative. He faced away from his patients so they could enter without distraction into a monologue of free association. In this way, Freud felt that the patient's buried, pathogenic memories would eventually, spontaneously surface to consciousness. Freud would then interpret the meaning of the patient's memories and dream images and their role in the origin of the patient's neurosis.

The Freudian ideal of detachment often produced psychoanalysts who were distracting simply by their lack of engagement. Their emotional reticence and their interpretations of their patients' lives often took on an authoritarian stance in which they seemed to be above and beyond any sort of emotional difficulty themselves, observing from on high their patients' anguish.

This detached, authoritarian attitude has been rejected in most contemporary forms of psychotherapy, as well as in relational innovations within psychoanalysis. Relational analysts coined the term "two-person" therapy to designate the recognition of the basic equality between the analyst and patient. Many therapists consider their own emotional responsiveness to be a crucial element in the psychotherapeutic process. These more contemporary forms of psychotherapy and psychoanalysis acknowledge that we can never completely suppress our personality or our true responses to the client, so analytic detachment is not even possible. Some relational modalities, such as Intersubjectivity Theory, developed by Robert Stolorow and George Atwood, go so far as to claim that even the client's narrative is "co-created" by the therapist and client. Even the client's memories are shaped in part by the therapist's collaboration and by the therapist's personal and cultural biases.

Yet, the relationship between the therapist and the client can also present the biggest challenges or even obstacles to the client's healing. If the therapist's emotional responses to the client are angry, shaming, envious, or sexual or if the therapist's relational style is withdrawn or intrusive, then the relationship may even be destructive for the client. Also, if the therapist's contact with themselves, and subsequently with others, lacks depth or cohesion, or if they live much more in one part of themselves than another, the relationship may be confusing and unsatisfying for the client. The client may not feel heard or received because of the limitations in the therapist's capacity for contact with another person.

The ability of the therapist to inhabit their own body and to know themselves as fundamental consciousness is therefore of key importance for the healing potential of the therapeutic relationship. When we inhabit our body, we are available to receive a client without either needing to shield ourselves or to come forward toward the client in order to feel connection. We can stay within the core of ourselves, connecting from the source of our love and intelligence. Although our experience will change and move in response to the client, we will remain a steady, quality-rich presence. Our intelligence and love will always be there, as part of the ongoing ground of our being, available for the client to rely upon.

We will also be grounded, in the sense of settled to the ground. By inhabiting our lower body, we cannot be as easily thrown off-base by the intensity of our client's emotions. Most clients will sense this and know that they can express the extremes of their anger, terror, or grief without overwhelming the therapist. They may also sense that they can embody their own full vitality, power, and intelligence without the therapist feeling threatened by them, as their own family may have felt when they were children.

Perhaps the most crucial element of a therapist's presence is our ability to feel compassion. Compassion is experienced as an innate capacity of embodiment. If we remain in contact with ourselves, compassion wells up within our body as a spontaneous response to the client's suffering.

The Therapist's Internal Responses to the Client

When we experience fundamental consciousness pervading ourselves and our client, we can be attuned to the client and ourselves at the same time. We can observe our own responses at the same time as we receive our client's presence and narrative. Our own personality, what we notice, and what we feel is important still influences the shape of our client's healing process. But we can more clearly observe when our responses to the client are based on our own psychological history or cultural biases. This means that we have less unconscious enmeshment with the client and less unconscious projection of our own biases onto their narrative. If we do react with anger, envy, or desire, we are immediately conscious of these reactions and can restrain ourselves from acting on them.

We can also discern our more subtle responses to the client. We may notice when we shield ourselves against the client's intensity by blocking our attunement to the unified space of fundamental consciousness. We may observe that we suddenly constrict our chest or hold our breath in order to obstruct our reception of the client. Or we may leave our own body in order to extend ourselves energetically toward the client in reaction to their distress. These are ordinary movements that we all experience in our interactions with other people; many are habitual, socially learned behaviors. However, the client may experience our shutting down as withdrawal from them or our energetic extension toward them as intrusion. When we are able to remain in contact with ourselves, we can remain open to the client without interfering with the flow of their healing process. We are disentangled from our client without being detached.

In this more spacious relationship, the client may experience more ability to attune inwardly to their own experience. Although it is also crucial to be seen and heard by another person, psychological healing is something that we really can only do for ourselves. It is an inward process of remembrance, self-examination, self-insight, and contact with the internal space of our own body. The therapist's stable, open presence gives the client permission and safety for this internal process. The therapist holds the thread that allows the client to make this solitary journey without fear of becoming lost in the labyrinth of their past.

The Therapist's Perception

The therapist who is attuned to the pervasive space of fundamental consciousness can, to some extent, "see-feel" the shifts in the client's experience as they speak. This can help us discern what is most potent for the client in their narrative, even if their words do not provide this emphasis. For example, a client may say that they feel very little about the loss of a parent, but the therapist will be able to observe the movement of grief or anger in the client's body even as they say this. They can also see-feel where the client is most open to experience and where they have defended themselves. Sometimes, they can even see the ages and the emotions that are held within the client's body.

There is an important difference between the way most sensitive people gather subtle information about their clients and the way fundamental consciousness allows us to know another person. Usually, sensitive people feel other people's pain in their own body. The pervasive space of FC enables us to see-feel the client's experience over there, within their body, without running it through our own body.

It is the capacity for direct knowing of another person's experience in our body that produces our tendency, as young children, to mirror our parent's pattern of openness and constriction. It causes us to feel, in our own body, whatever grief, anger, or anxiety is in our childhood environment as if it were our own feeling. As children, we are extremely impressionable to the experience of other people. We have not yet matured in our inward contact with ourselves or in our ability to discern and name what we are experiencing in our environment. We therefore have very little ability to distinguish our own internal experience from the other internal experience of other people.

Many sensitive people retain this direct knowing of other people's experience as adults. They are particularly sensitive to the emotional experience of other people, either because of their innate gifts of sensitivity or because traumatic experiences in childhood have kept them in an enmeshed or a hypervigilant state with their surroundings (or both). People who are sensitive to the pain of other people are often drawn to the helping professions. Many psychotherapists report that they can feel what others are feeling, not just be reading changes of expression of posture but by actually feeling the other person's feelings in their own body. They may also describe some discomfort at this and exhaustion at the end of a day of working with people in pain. This entrainment, or mirroring of another person's pain, can also be confusing. If we experience another person's pain in our own body, it can be difficult to distinguish their pain from our own.

As fundamental consciousness, however, the therapist is attuned to themselves and the client in a way that is deeper, or more subtle, than mirroring or entrainment. Instead of feeling the client's pain in our own body, we can see and feel it within the client's body. Although we may respond with the same emotion in our own body, we can discern that it is our own response to the other person, rather than that person's emotion. And we may respond with some other emotion. As the pervasive space of FC, we can know what we are experiencing in our own body and what the other person is experiencing in their body at the same time. Empathy occurs across distance, rather than by feeling the client's suffering as if it were our own.

The Healing Process

As the basis of the therapeutic relationship, fundamental consciousness encompasses both the separate individuality and the oneness of the therapist and the client at the same time. The openness and authentic presence of both the therapist and the client seems to produce a spontaneous, and often mutual, healing process. As therapists, we can learn to trust this process to emerge. We do not have to fill the silence with ideas or healing strategies. We can open to the silence and allow the true creativity of the situation to flow.

As Freud observed many years ago, the painful memories of the client seem to follow their own order; they emerge in exactly the right sequence for the client to be able to understand and resolve them. The client may also become aware of the constrictions and fragmentations in their body as they relate the narrative of their psychological history, and these rigidities may become more visible for the therapist as the client is ready to release them.

The therapeutic process is often healing for both the client and the therapist. Many therapists report that their clients bring issues to therapy that are also key psychological issues of their own. And that helping the client resolve these issues contributes to their own healing.

Or that the client's expression of pain helps dislodge and release the pain in their own body. The practice of sitting in the open space of fundamental consciousness while another person expresses their deepest wounding can also help us open our heart and our understanding, and become stable in our realization of fundamental consciousness.

To stabilize in one's realization of fundamental consciousness means that the pervasive space is always there, pervading our body and environment. Not that we are always aware of it, but if we check on it, there it is. We do not need to shift our perspective or attune to it, or even find it—it is just there.

As fundamental consciousness, we are naturally equal with our client. Situated in the core of our body means that we are living within the center of our being. And the center of our own being is also the center—it touches and connects with the center—of all other beings. We cannot inhabit our body fully and know ourselves as fundamental consciousness, if we are holding ourselves either above or below other people.

At first, in the therapeutic process, it is usually just the therapist who has realized fundamental consciousness. But, as the client continues to do the Realization Process practices and to release holding patterns from their body, they will gradually join the therapist in the experience of pervasive space and oneness. The contact between the therapist and the client will be experienced throughout the internal space of both bodies, both beings. Love meets love, not in the space between two people, but within each person's chest. Understanding meets understanding, as a felt experience, a resonance, within each person's body.

Part II: Applying the Realization Process to Specific Psychological Categories

The guide for diagnosing psychological ailments that most students of psychotherapy study is called the *Diagnostic and Statistical Manual of Mental Disorders (DSM)*. It has a section called "personality disorders." This includes obsessive-compulsive, schizoid, avoidant, dependent, borderline, histrionic, antisocial, paranoid, schizotypal, and narcissistic personality disorders. These are categories of behavior. Each one of these types of behavior appears on a spectrum from mild to severe. On the severe end, they are most clearly delineated and more difficult (although not impossible) to treat. But on the mild end, they are very common—most of us have some amount of one or several of these types of behavior.

Just as with the constrictions in our body, we formed these behavioral patterns as ways of coping with painful events and relationships in our childhood and by mirroring the behavior of our parents. These types of behaviors are usually augmented and sustained by chronic patterns of tension in the body. This appendix looks at how the Realization Process practices can assist in the healing of a few of these "personality disorders." I have chosen to describe the application of the Realization Process to the histrionic, obsessive-compulsive, and narcissistic personality disorders as the RP practices have been particularly effective in their treatment. Treatment of the avoidant and schizoid personality disorders can also be facilitated with the relational practices provided in chapter 7.

Classifications, such as those in the DSM, are generally too limited to encompass the complexity of personality and the creativity of our coping mechanisms. There is a danger that therapists who rely on these diagnoses may produce preconceived treatment plans that do not recognize or address the specific design of their clients' personality difficulties. On the positive side, labeling categories of behavior can sometimes help people accept themselves and others. Self-acceptance is an important step in releasing a pattern—we cannot make a change in something that we try to ignore or deny.

Even more spiritually oriented methods of classification, such as astrology and the enneagram, depending on how they are used, may have some of the same problems and benefits as the DSM categories. They can help us understand and accept ourselves, but they can also limit our horizons of change and growth. Although these methods do not pathologize categories of behavior, as the DSM does, they sometimes make the assigned categories seem less flexible than in the DSM. As static categories, they can prevent us from knowing ourselves and others directly and specifically, beyond the label.

Rigid patterns of behavior hold us in old relationships with the world, which were formed in our childhood. The embodiment and oneness practices of the Realization Process can aid in the healing of any of the so-called personality disorders by helping people deepen contact with themselves and others. As we become authentically ourselves, our behavior becomes more spontaneous, and our personality becomes more fluid and wider in scope.

Histrionic Personality Disorder

Histrionic personality disorder is a diagnosis given to people who are extremely dramatic in the way they express themselves, who crave attention, and who are often very emotional. A few years ago, I worked with a woman named Louise who could be diagnosed with this disorder. Almost everything she said was an exaggeration and expressed with intense facial expressions, dramatic vocal inflection, and suspenseful pauses. She locked eyes with me when she spoke, as if to hammer home to me whatever she was saying. If I looked away from her for a moment, she would amplify her voice and mannerisms. I found it hard not to look away from her, as her contrived way of communicating was so grating. She was also, of course, terribly lonely, because most people found her abrasive. And when people backed away from her, she knew no way of trying to hold on to them except to further exaggerate her voice, her focus, and her gestures. This produced a vicious relational cycle of amplifying her expression to try to connect with people who were rejecting her because of her amplified expression.

Although my impulse was to pull back from her exaggerated posturing, my attunement to fundamental consciousness, pervading us both, allowed me to stay open with her. I could feel stable within myself and allow her to be just as she was without closing off my connection with her. This began to calm her almost immediately. She sensed that it might take less effort for her to be seen in this situation, and that it might be safer for her to be seen. For she was terrified of both—not being seen and being seen. Her dramatic posturing was both a beacon and a shield.

She relaxed her delivery somewhat as she described to me a childhood of feeling completely ignored and even invisible. She was somewhere in the middle of eight children, and their house was always filled with noise and chaos. Her father was gone at work and then at the bar most of the day and evening, leaving her mother alone, overwhelmed, and depressed as she attempted to cope with the children.

Louise remembered standing at the curb outside their home, dancing, and singing, hoping to attract the attention of people in a passing car so that they might take her away with them. Luckily, that never happened. But she felt that she had spent her whole life trying to attract attention and failing. "I feel like I'm performing, even when I'm alone," she said.

Inhabiting her body was a revelation for her. The first time she was able to experience herself in her body, she cried out, "There is someone in here. There really is. I can feel myself!" She had become used to being just a portrayal of a person, rather than an actual person. Although she had put so much effort into trying to be noticed, her fear of being seen was that people would see that there was no one there.

Of course it took a while, but Louise very gradually became adept at living within her body and feeling relaxed within herself. She also practiced allowing people to see into her, receiving the gaze of other people within her body, rather than projecting herself out toward them. "It feels so much gentler," she said. As was to be expected, from a lifetime of exaggerating her speech, there was a great deal of constriction within her throat. This was relieved through the release technique of focusing within the tension, allowing it to move further into constriction, then letting go, and then inhabiting the area. She also practiced staying within her whole body as she spoke. It was difficult for her to believe that she could make any impact with her words if she did not send them out into the world with force. But one day, she made a discovery that thrilled her. "My voice is connected to my heart," she said. "I can feel and speak at the same time. I can speak from my heart." Now she felt that it did not even matter if people did not listen to her or understand her. "I am saying what I know is true," she said. "And I'm just leaving space for them to listen if they want to."

Obsessive-Compulsive Personality Disorder

Obsessive-compulsive personality disorder (OCPD) is a personality structure in which a person is overly concerned with perfection, control, and attention to details. It may also include hoarding, procrastination, and difficulty with completing projects. Obsessive-compulsive behaviors are generally rooted in anxiety. Releasing the holding patterns in the body associated with this personality pattern can help uncover the origins of the anxiety and resolve it.

Peter came to work with me because he was trying to write a book but was unable to complete it because it never seemed ready. His continual rewriting of each page made progress very slow. He often interrupted his work in order to reorganize his computer files, putting them in ever more perfect arrangements.

He also suffered from "information hoarding," a type of hoarding that is often a symptom of OCPD. He spent many hours researching and collecting masses of data about any household item that he needed to purchase to make sure that he could find the best deal and the most efficient products. He often felt that utility companies were overcharging or in other ways taking advantage of him. He said that he had cartons of bills and records of his payments going back for decades that he could not bring himself to throw out.

Peter's obsessive thinking had produced a rigid tension in his forehead. Many people have tension in their forehead from a lifetime of worry or of forcing themselves to concentrate. A common pattern is to squeeze the sides of the forehead inward. Peter's tension took the form of a thickened ridge above and between his brows. When he focused within this tension, he could feel that it related to his chronic worry about being cheated. As he allowed the tension pattern to move further into constriction and then release, he also remembered that his father had held his forehead in the same way and that his father's forehead would become more constricted if he were worried about money. Peter could feel how he mirrored his father's tension.

As he let this pattern release, he felt that he was also healing his father. He felt the legacy of strain of the male role to support his family. He recognized that his obsessive fear of being cheated or of making the

195

wrong purchase was, at root, a fear of failing as a man that had been passed down from father to son. Even though he was not the sole provider in his adult family and he and his wife were living comfortably, this old fear was still imprinted in him.

As the tension in his forehead began to release, he felt great relief, and his fears of being taken advantage of and of financial failure dwindled. He also felt increased contact with his whole head. He was able to inhabit his whole brain, not just his forehead. He reported that this made thinking much easier. "The thoughts just happen," he said. "When I have a problem to solve now, I just wait, and the solution pops up in my mind. I don't have to keep chewing on it." He also found that he was able to concentrate better and to allow himself to move forward through his writing project. "It's a matter of trust," he said. He even began to throw out some of his hoards of bills and records. He told me, "I'm just doing it a little at a time."

Narcissistic Personality Disorder

In the more extreme range of narcissistic personality disorder, the person is described as having such an expanded sense of their own importance that they have no empathy for other people. They live in their own bubble, a world that entirely centers on them and that exists only to cater to their needs and admire their grandeur. This inflation is usually accompanied by intense reactions to real or imagined insults. The narcissist's susceptibility to insult can also slide toward more severe paranoid fantasy in which their importance (and their underlying extreme vulnerability) makes them the imagined target of menacing conspiracies.

However, in its milder forms, narcissism is a very common human ailment. Just as in its more severe form, it is based on emotional wounding, early in life, to our budding sense of self and self-esteem. It is the way that we compensate for deficiency in our normal self-love.

Children, with their limited scope of experience, naturally feel that the world revolves around them. If they are well cared for, all their needs are met immediately. They feel hunger, and the breast or the bottle arrives in their mouth. They feel sleepy, and they are tucked in and kissed good night. By this same token, children also tend to blame themselves for any misfortune to themselves or to their family. They are the main protagonist in the unfolding story of their lives. Only gradually does the child's horizon expand to include an awareness of the needs, accomplishments, and perspectives of other people.

In a healthy maturation process, our own contact with ourselves and the natural sense of esteem and self-love that accompanies this inward contact also matures as we grow to accommodate and appreciate other people. A traumatic disruption to this process may result in a pattern of disregard for our own needs in order to accommodate the needs of others. Or it may result in the compensatory pattern of the narcissistic inflation of our needs and a disregard for the needs of others.

All children have moments of shame, usually the result of criticism or derision from those they love or their own self-judgement of failure. The prevalence and intensity of these moments, and our own native sensitivity to the way people react to us, will determine how deeply these experiences affect our self-esteem and self-love. Many people grow up with some degree of self-doubt, or even self-loathing, and compensate by developing mild narcissistic patterns. For example, we may work hard to perfect ourselves, or at least to present an image of perfection to other people, and then feel bitter humiliation when this image is challenged. We may compare ourselves to others, constantly weighing our own worth against the accomplishments of other people. We may find that our happiness and confidence depend upon the reassurance of other people and wanes when that reassurance is not available.

Once in a workshop, we were talking about the tendency to feel either superior or inferior to other people depending on the circumstances. We decided to find the somatic organizations for these common relational patterns. Partners took turns feeling superior to the other person, then inferior, and then equal. We found that the feelings of superiority, inferiority, or equality were expressed in a distinct raising, lowering, or relaxing of bodily organization. Although just a slight movement, there was an obvious looking down on the other person or up to the other person that expressed the superior and inferior attitudes. As in all organizations, these bodily patterns obstructed actual contact with oneself and with the other person. For many people, the raised or lowered attitude is a rigid, unconsciously held pattern, chronically separating them from other people.

Narcissistic patterns are also often visible in an inflation or lifting of the chest, an actual "puffing out" of the torso. Although this appears as an expansion of the chest, or of the whole torso, it is held in place by chronic tightening of the muscles and fascia. This rigidly held pattern keeps us from experiencing the authentic qualities of our actual power and self-esteem within our body.

Just as with all the rigid patterns of personality and behavior, the narcissistic disorder can be healed by making actual contact with ourselves. When we inhabit our body, we can experience our authentic being beneath our false posturing and social masks. And this being is naturally open to other people. Wherever we are in contact with the internal space of the body, we are open and responsive to our environment. The qualities of our being are an important part of our self-enjoyment. When we experience them, our need to inflate ourselves or to compare ourselves with others diminishes. We feel complete within ourselves.

NOTES

Introduction: The Undivided Light

Opening quote. Aura Glaser, "Weavings," December 21, 2017, auraglaser.com/news/.

Chapter 1: How We Organize Ourselves

Opening quote. Yehuda Amichai, "Huleikat" in *Yehuda Amichai: A Life of Poetry 1948–1994*, trans. Benjamin and Barbara Harshav (New York: HarperCollins Publishers, 1994), 411.

Chapter 2: Fundamental Consciousness

Opening quote. Joan Stambaugh, *The Formless Self* (Albany: State University of New York Press, 1999), 79.
1. Keiji Nishitani, *Religion and Nothingness* (Berkeley and Los Angeles: University of California Press, 1982).

Chapter 3: Inhabiting the Body

1. Elizabeth F. Howell, *The Dissociative Mind* (New York: Routledge, 2005).

Chapter 4: The Qualities in the Body

Opening quote. Keiji Nishitani, *Religion and Nothingness* (Berkeley and Los Angeles: University of California Press, 1982), 164.

Chapter 5: Healing Trauma from the Core of the Body

Opening quote. Joan Stambaugh, *The Formless Self* (Albany: State University of New York Press, 1999), 95.

Chapter 6: Freeing the Senses from Trauma

Opening quote. Paul Muller-Ortega, *The Triadic Heart of Shiva* (Albany: State University of New York, 1989), 182.

Chapter 7: Relationships

Opening quote. Elizabeth F. Howell, *The Dissociative Mind* (New York: Routledge, 2005), 4.

1. Jaideva Singh, trans., *Vijnanabhairava* (Delhi: Motilal Banarsidass Publishers, 1979).
2. Paul Muller-Ortega, *The Triadic Heart of Shiva* (Albany: State University of New York, 1989), 122.
3. Joyce Edward, Nathene Ruskin, and Patsy Turrini, *Separation-Individuation* (New York: Gardner Press, 1981).
4. Daniel N. Stern, *The Interpersonal World of the Infant* (New York: Basic Books, 1985).
5. Edward, Ruskin, and Turrini, *Separation-Individuation*.

Chapter 8: The Realization Process Release Technique

Opening quote. Lewis Aron, "The Clinical Body and the Reflexive Mind," in Lewis Aron and Frances Sommer Anderson, *Relational Perspectives on the Body* (Hillsdale, NJ: The Analytic Press, 1998), 4.

Chapter 9: Toward Healing Anxiety and Depression

Opening quote. Ramana Maharshi, *Talks with Ramana Maharshi* (Carslbad, CA: Inner Directions Foundation, 2000), 138.

Chapter 10: Trauma and Spiritual Teachings

Opening quote. Yuasa Yasuo, *The Body* (Albany: State University of New York Press, 1987), 156.

1. Irmgard Schloegl, trans., *The Zen Teachings of Rinzai* (Berkeley: Shambhala, 1976), 22.
2. Schloegl, *The Zen Teachings*, 22.

ABOUT THE AUTHOR

Judith Blackstone, PhD, is an innovative spiritual teacher and a psychotherapist with four decades of clinical experience. She developed the Realization Process, an embodied approach to personal and relational healing and nondual spiritual realization. She is author of *Belonging Here, The Intimate Life, The Enlightenment Process,* and *The Empathic Ground.* For more information on the Realization Process or for Judith's teaching itinerary, visit judithblackstone.com.

ABOUT SOUNDS TRUE

S ounds True is a multimedia publisher whose mission is to inspire and support personal transformation and spiritual awakening. Founded in 1985 and located in Boulder, Colorado, we work with many of the leading spiritual teachers, thinkers, healers, and visionary artists of our time. We strive with every title to preserve the essential "living wisdom" of the author or artist. It is our goal to create products that not only provide information to a reader or listener, but that also embody the quality of a wisdom transmission.

For those seeking genuine transformation, Sounds True is your trusted partner. At SoundsTrue.com you will find a wealth of free resources to support your journey, including exclusive weekly audio interviews, free downloads, interactive learning tools, and other special savings on all our titles.

To learn more, please visit SoundsTrue.com/freegifts or call us toll-free at 800.333.9185.